CONCILIUM

THEOLOGY IN THE AGE OF RENEWAL

CONCILIUM

EXECUTIVE EDITORIAL COMMITTEE

EXECUTIVE SECRETARY

Marcel Vanhengel, O.P.
Arksteestraat 3
Nijmegen, Netherlands

EDITORIAL DIRECTORS

Edward Schillebeeckx, O.P., *Nijmegen, Netherlands* (Dogma)
Johannes Wagner, *Trier, W. Germany* (Liturgy)
Karl Rahner, S.J., *Munich, W. Germany* (Pastoral Theology)
Hans Küng, *Tübingen, W. Germany* (Ecumenical Theology)
Franz Böckle, *Bonn, W. Germany* (Moral Theology)
Johannes Metz, *Münster, W. Germany* (Fundamental Theology)
Roger Aubert, *Louvain, Belgium* (Church History)
Teodoro Jiménez-Urresti, *Bilbao, Spain* (Canon Law)
✠ Neophytos Edelby, *Damascus, Syria* (Canon Law)
Christian Duquoc, O.P., *Lyons, France* (Spirituality)
Pierre Benoit, O.P., *Jerusalem, Jordan* (Sacred Scripture)
Roland Murphy, O. Carm., *Washington, D.C.* (Sacred Scripture)

CONSULTING EDITORS

Leo Alting von Geusau, *Groningen, Netherlands*
Ludolph Baas, *Amersfoort, Netherlands*
✠ Carlo Colombo, *Varese, Italy*
Yves Congar, O.P., *Strasbourg, France*
Charles A. Davis, *Heythrop, England*
Godfrey Diekmann, O.S.B., *Collegeville, Minn.*
Henri de Lubac, S.J., *Lyons, France*
Jorge Mejía, *Buenos Aires, Argentina*
Mateus Cardoso Peres, O.P., *Fatima, Portugal*

CONCILIUM / VOL. 14

ECUMENICAL THEOLOGY

DO WE KNOW THE OTHERS?

Volume 14

1-0315

CONCILIUM
theology in the age of renewal

PAULIST PRESS
NEW YORK, N.Y. / GLEN ROCK, N.J.

Copyright © 1966 by
Paulist Fathers, Inc. and Stichting Concilium

All Rights Reserved
Nothing contained in this publication shall be duplicated and/or made public by means of print, photography, microfilm, or in any other manner, without the previous consent of Paulist Press and Stichting Concilium.

Library of Congress Catalogue Card Number: 66-20895

Suggested Decimal Classification: 280.1

BOOK DESIGN: Claude Ponsot

Paulist Press assumes responsibility for the accuracy of the English translations in this Volume.

PAULIST PRESS
EXECUTIVE OFFICES: 304 W. 58th Street, New York, N.Y. and 21 Harristown Road, Glen Rock, N.J.
Executive Publisher: John A. Carr, C.S.P.
Executive Manager: Alvin A. Illig, C.S.P.
Asst. Executive Manager: Thomas E. Comber, C.S.P.

EDITORIAL OFFICES: 304 W. 58th Street, New York, N.Y.
Editor: Kevin A. Lynch, C.S.P.
Managing Editor: Urban P. Intondi

Printed and bound in the United States of America by
The Colonial Press Inc., Clinton, Mass.

CONTENTS

PART II

BIBLIOGRAPHICAL SURVEY

PART III

DOCUMENTATION CONCILIUM

Hans Küng/*Tübingen, W. Germany*

Preface

D o we really know the others? If we are honest with ourselves, we have to admit that we do not. But we have begun to know them, and that is already a great step forward. It implies at least that we are interested in getting to know them. And yet, this was not always so. For many centuries we had no desire to know them—or, if we did, it was only a desire to know them from the worst side so that we could at once defeat and dispose of them with theological arguments. Today we are interested in getting to know them because they, too, are *Christians* and *Christian* Churches, in a genuine and often better sense. And should we not be concerned with knowing our own brethren?

For they *are* our brethren, even though they differ from us in many ways. Diversity is often more fruitful than unity in mediocrity. We should be particularly concerned about this because, for all their weaknesses and the one-sidedness from which they, too, obviously suffer, there are many things they do *better* as Christians than we. We notice this as soon as we begin to know them. It then begins to dawn upon us that so often our catholicity is unfortunately not a reality but only a possibility, a claim, a program which *still demands* fulfillment. But the others have already *put into practice* many of the points of this program, albeit very often in a selective and narrow way. Is it necessary to mention their appreciation of Holy Scripture in theology

1

and in practice, their lively and intelligible religious services and their great achievements in theology? To get to know the others, then, means to *learn* from them, and as we learn from them, we make ourselves better known to them. As long as we did not understand them, they could not understand us, and vice versa.

Obviously, we do not learn blindly. We can hardly take everything for granted. However, we can test everything. "Test *everything;* hold fast what is *good*" (1 Thess. 5, 21). We have been given a criterion by which to judge others (and ourselves): the original message of Jesus Christ, the Lord of the Church and the apostolic Church that originally bore witness to him.

This volume of CONCILIUM seeks to help in this understanding of the others in the spirit of Vatican Council II. It contains only a small choice of problems that are relevant here, but they are, we hope, representative problems that may pin down some decisive points in the present state of the discussion. In this, we are not only considering the present but also, at least insofar as the Protestant Reformation is concerned, the past which determines the character of the present often more than the present by itself. Thus, we have to consider Luther and Calvin before we turn to the present day. It was therefore obvious that we should call upon Orthodox and Evangelical authors for the treatment of Orthodox and Evangelical subjects, while Catholic theologians would try to meet them from the point of view of Catholic theology. For too long we (and the others) have told ourselves and the others what they are instead of simply *asking* *them.*

In this volume it should become obvious to anyone not yet aware of it that, after Vatican Council II, theology still has a great deal more to do, not less. At the same time, theology has become more exciting, a true adventure of the spirit, and worth the best we can give. And yet, there is also more hope and joy in theology since it can again help man today in many things. This awakening of Catholic theology to a new life is one of those immensely far-reaching results of the Council which are real, even if they find little mention in the Decrees.

PART I
ARTICLES

Erwin Iserloh/*Trèves, France*

Luther in Contemporary Catholic Thought

I

A MANY-SIDED PERSONALITY

The progress of the ecumenical movement has shown that efforts for the reunion of Christians cannot be effective unless history is taken into account. To do so is to clear away much debris, to throw into relief the historical limits of many deep-rooted questions and so bring them up-to-date and into better focus. Personalities, who, with the passage of time, have been distorted by hostility and bias or rendered falsely heroic, can only be understood when they have been set in the proper light against the background of their own time. This is primarily true of Martin Luther, who gave the Reformation—especially in Germany—its peculiar stamp. If the image of the reformer has been a controversial one up to the present, it is so not only because judgment on his personality and work is tied up with the believer's decision on the Reformation's claim to truth: Luther is for some the champion of the faith, for others he is a heretic and the destroyer of Church unity. Actually, the root of the difficulty we experience in reaching the person and the work and in representing both with truthfulness lies in Luther himself.

We have a great mass of Luther's own writings and of his own personal witness to himself and his intentions. There is, to be sure, an inner consistency to these writings. All his questions

5

basically stem from a very few historical points. But he has not—
as Calvin did in his *Institutions*—left us any systematic work or
a complete presentation of his theology. In fact, he was very
much restricted by events and the controversy of the moment. His
works consist in articles written for particular occasions; they
are lectures, debates, sermons. Moreover, in his progress from
monk to reformer, he experienced a profound change. Because
his method was closely bound up with his experience, he was
unable to see in retrospect the earlier phases of his development
without prejudice. Therefore, he has himself contributed in large
measure to the establishment of a "Luther legend", which only in
the last decade, thanks to the painstaking work of men like Otto
Scheel,[1] has been dismantled piece by piece.

Moreover, everything that Luther wrote is a confession paid
for with his own experience and his own suffering, which he
felt obliged to share with others. In the course of this compulsive
sharing, he does not shrink from strong terms to make his meaning clear; indeed, in Luther's writings, paradox becomes a style
commensurate with the author. No wonder then that he suc-
cumbs too often to the dangers inherent in his irascible tempera-
ment and his polemical power.

All this makes it difficult to comprehend the convolutions of
his nature and the richness of his works; it also makes it possible
for him to appear wavering and inconsistent over and over again.
Luther's contemporary, Johannes Cochlaeus, had already noted
this fact and called him "Luther septiceps" (Hydra-headed
Luther), and he sought to confute him from his own writings.

If Heinrich Boehmer can say with justice: "There are as many
Luthers as there are books from Luther's pen,"[2] the reason is not
only that different viewers have created a picture of the reformer
suited to the theology and the piety of their time; rather, the picture is a composite in keeping with the spiritual makeup of the
original. Again, Luther's many-sided and many-leveled character

---

[1] O. Scheel, *Martin Luther. Vom Katholizismus zur Reformation* (2
Vols.) (Tübingen, [3]1921/1930).
[2] H. Boehmer, *Luther im Lichte der neueren Forschung* (Leipzig,
[5]1918), p. 5.

brings with it the possibility and the peril that from time to time a line or a theme will be explored and isolated from the rest of his work: perhaps stressing forensic justification at the expense of inner renewal, which he surely represented, or his theology of the Word as the essential, and his adherence to the sacrament as inconsequential, as fundamentally the undigested residue of Catholicism; or seeing him as revolutionary in his defiant and bold remonstrance to Pope and Council, and the development of the national Church as deviating from the properly Protestant tendency; or, finally, to see the statement of Schleiermacher: "The Reformation is still going on!" as the legitimate interpretation of Luther's desire, and, on the contrary, to see the orthodoxy of the 16th and the 19th centuries as a falsification of Luther's legacy, even though it may be able, in every instance, to quote Luther *materialiter* to support its positions.

II

A Change in the Catholic Image of Luther

Though we may speak of a change in the Protestant image of Luther, of "Luther in the Transformation of His Church",[3] the Catholic representation has remained tolerably constant through all the centuries up to the threshold of our own period. It remained "under the spell of Cochlaeus's commentary",[4] as Adolf Herte has demonstrated in his three-volume work. According to this account of the struggle, which Johannes Cochlaeus drafted in 1549, three years after the death of the reformer, Luther was for Catholics simply the heretic who, by his false teaching, had plunged uncounted souls into ruin; he was the destroyer of the Church's unity, the demagogue, the man who brought misery and want to Germany and to Christendom from the Peasants'

[3] H. Stephan, *Luther in den Wandlungen seiner Kirche* (Berlin, [2]1951).
[4] A. Herte, *Das katholische Lutherbild im Bann der Lutherkommentare des Cochlaeus* (3 Vols.) (Münster, 1943); J. Cochlaeus, *Commentarii de actis et scriptis Martini Lutheri* (1549).

War onward. Into this one-sided and somber picture, at the beginning of the 19th century Johann Adam Möhler introduced some brighter colors, praising Luther's vigorous piety, and admitting that the fullness of Luther's sublime thought could have edified the Church if Luther himself had not ruptured her unity by his presumption and demagoguery.[5]

The intensification of confessional opposition in Germany since the mid-19th century prevented any follow-up of Möhler's attempt to revise Luther's image. Not until historical scholarship, which considers objectivity and fidelity to sources as its highest duty, and which, in the field of Catholicism, sought to obtain recognition for the Görresgesellschaft (Görres Society), was a change brought about. A first pioneer in this matter was Sebastian Merkle (1862-1945).[6] In his case, I admit, there was no conscious ecumenical motivation. But he would wish to see Luther —whom he "unequivocally held to be wholly anti-Catholic" [7] —historically justified and his good intentions recognized. He saw it as a problem for the psychologist and the historian that Luther, who "objectively was wrong", "must be understood subjectively".[8] How unprepared the rank and file of laity and clergy were to accept this at the beginning of the century (1902) is shown by the Beyhl-Berlichingen lawsuit in Würzburg in which Merkle was involved.

Semi-scholarly lectures for the general public on "The Reformation, Revolution, and the Thirty Years' War" by Baron Adolf von Berlichingen had, by false claims and extravagant statements, stirred up confessional passions and brought charges

[5] J. A. Möhler, *Kirchengeschichte*, III, edited by P. Gams, O.S.B. (Regensburg, 1868), pp. 100-8.

[6] See his articles "Wiederum das Lutherproblem," "Luthers Quellen," "Das Lutherbild der Gegenwart," "Gutes an Luther und Übles an seinen Tadlern," "Zu Heinrich Denifle, Luther," now in *Sebastian Merkle: Ausgewählte Reden und Aufsätze* (T. Freudenberger, ed.): *Quellen und Forschungen zur Geschichte des Bistums und Hochstifts Würzburg*, 17 (Würzburg, 1965).

[7] J. Lortz, *op. cit.*, pp. 57-96; 86.

[8] *Das Lutherbild in der Gegenwart, ibid.*, p. 226.

of "ultra-montane falsifications of history" from the Protestant Professor Beyhl. A suit grew out of this charge, calling upon the aforementioned Sebastian Merkle, the local Church historian, as an authority. He declared that Berlichingen's statements about Luther were false and denied him any scientific authority. This verdict gave annoyance in Catholic circles; it was felt to be a "stab in the back" of the Catholic position. People were not willing to accept the fact that they had been proved to be prejudiced not by Merkle but by Berlichingen, and it was necessary to put Catholic historical research above suspicion by clear demonstration of the truth.

In 1903, the year of the trial, there appeared the huge work on Luther, *Luther und Luthertum,* by the long-time Assistant Archivist of the Vatican Archives, the Dominican Heinrich Denifle. This work dropped a bomb into the veneration for Luther current at the end of the 19th century. It was not a biography but a series of learned probings into two problem areas: "The Evolution of Luther as a Reformer", and "Luther and Scholasticism". Of permanent value in this out-of-date work is its history of dogma. In an impressive fashion, Denifle had pointed out Luther's dependence upon the Nominalism to be found in the later Scholasticism. If, to be sure, he reproached Luther with not knowing Thomas, or that he misunderstood him just as he had misunderstood Augustine and Bernard (and this, for the disputatious Tyrolean, is equivalent to dishonesty), he did not sufficiently take into account what was the particular style of thought of the late Scholastics and what was new in Luther. "To reproach a non-Dominican in those days for not knowing Thomas and not following him, would be as absurd as to dispute the professional competence of a master-builder of the baroque period because he did not build in the Gothic style." [9]

As far as Luther's early development is concerned, Denifle forced Protestant research to prove the utterances of the later Luther and to understand them more as the result of his Catholic

[9] *Ibid.,* p. 206.

premises. In many Protestant works, notably in the great work of Otto Scheel, *Martin Luther. Vom Katholizismus zur Reformation,* this has borne fruit.

The undisputed scientific importance of Denifle's work remains, but opposed to it is his unbridled speech, his malicious ill-will toward the reformer in whose person he could see only the dark side, viewing his doctrine of justification and his struggle against the monastic vows only as the offshoot of personal moral depravity; for Denifle only the lies, the falsifications and the calumnies were confirmed, and for him in every case *bona fides* was denied. In short, "this book was a moral and scientific execution of the renegade Augustinian by the true-blue Dominican" (Jedin). In one widely acclaimed review of 1904—but not often understood by his contemporaries—Merkle blamed the tone of the work, but at the same time showed the importance of its contents.

The Jesuit, Hartmann Grisar, in his three-volume work *Luther* (1911-12), and in his one-volume biography of Luther, *Martin Luthers Leben und Werk* (1926), has avoided Denifle's coarseness. He points out, as occasion demands, the reformer's good sides, and he clears up many of the "Luther legends" of both camps. He concentrates more on the psychological than the dogmatic aspects, and even undertakes a psycho-pathological interpretation of his subject. Although Grisar's treatment of Luther is detailed and his demonstration is sound throughout, he still has not really come to grips with what is peculiar to Luther: the religious motivation. Indeed, he disavows the religious motive; nowhere in Luther's case does he discover any true piety. For this reason and in spite of his admirable scholarship, he remains superficial. Nevertheless, Merkle sees Grisar's work as an advance over Denifle, the first, especially, who rectified the earlier Catholic judgment on Luther, and he derives from it the "consoling certainty that little by little a more valid appreciation is growing of the role of Catholic scholarship, no longer considering that scholar to be the best Catholic who believes that he can enhance the authority of his Church in the eyes of outsiders by one-sided, absolute condemnation of the adversary and by equally one-sided adulation of the less gratifying aspects of Catholicism." [10]

III

NEW CATHOLIC IMAGE OF LUTHER

The expectation aroused by Merkle has been realized in the work of Joseph Lortz. In his *Kirchengeschichte in ideengeschichtlicher Betrachtung*[11] and in *Die Reformation in Deutschland*,[12] he has sketched a picture of Luther and the Reformation which both Catholics and Protestants will perceive to be a turning point. At the same time, he has contributed in a real way to a change in climate in the situation of the Confessional Churches in the last decade. In absolute submission where dogma is concerned, he wants to "say the truth in charity".

For Lortz, the situation of the Church on the eve of the Reformation was one of manifold abuses, of such extensive theological confusion and of such religious weakness, that after so many favorable opportunities for reform had been bypassed, the Reformation, in the sense of a revolution within the Church, had become unavoidable. Hence, there is a considerable Catholic share in the guilt for the resulting division of the Church at the time of the Reformation. After tremendous inner struggle before God, Martin Luther outgrew the Roman Church. As a reformer, he was unwillingly locked in a struggle with an unsatisfactory presentation of Catholicism. He "overcame" in himself a Catholicism which was not Catholic (I, 76), and he "had discovered, as a heretic, the great treasure of Catholicism" (I, 434). Whatever other meanings may be ascribed to Luther, he was a religious man and a great man of prayer (I, 383). He lived in a trusting submission to the heavenly Father through the Crucified. The formal rule was "sola fide" (I, 385). Therefore, he struggled

[10] *Ibid.*, p. 211.
[11] 22./23. (1964).
[12] 1939; 4th ed. (1962).

against the notion of "justification through good works". His religious desires were met by the deputies of the Church, of the pope and the bishops, without the necessary gravity and requisite responsibility.

These confirmations do not prevent Lortz from exercising with regard to Luther his own severe critical faculty. He finds Luther to be strongly influenced by events; he is unbridled, immoderate, romantic, indeed sensual. A man of his type has to "conquer" reality; he cannot accept it with moderation and humility; therefore, he is not in the full sense of the word a "hearer" of God's Word, not completely a hearer of the Bible, nor, in fact, completely submissive to the Church. In short, from the very roots of his being, Luther is subjective. It is clear that this critic takes a middle position; he is more difficult to dismiss than the insolent Denifle and the coldly analytic Grisar. But it is characteristic of the change in the climate of thought that the matter has come to the stage of a comprehensive interconfessional discussion, in which, even though harsh criticism and rejection persist, Luther is no longer vilified.

The Evangelical Church historian, Erwin Mülhaupt, a few years ago sought to diminish the significance of Lortz's work by his remark that it is not representative of Catholic thought today. He writes: "We must, it seems to me, increase the difference (*viz.* between Lortz and Przywara), lest at this time we accept as the Catholic position on the Reformation the view which Professor Lortz accepts—a gratifying and comforting one, to be sure. Unfortunately, we cannot assume it to be the authoritative Catholic attitude . . . We cannot, unfortunately, perceive anything of this spirit in authoritative, papal Catholicism up to the present day." [13] No one can be entirely in disagreement with this; permission for a new edition of *Reformation in Deutschland* was refused. Since then, not only has it been published (1962), but the fresh approach begun with the Pontificate of John XXIII and developed during the Council is evident in the *Decree on*

---

[13] Lortz, "Luther und der Papst," in *Materialdienst des konfessionskundlichen Instituts* 7 (1956), pp. 108ff.

Ecumenism. Here Catholics are invited to recognize the riches of Christ and the virtuous works in the lives of their separated brethren (n. 4), and the fact was emphasized that the schism had come about, "for which, often enough, men of both sides were to blame" (n. 3). This means, as Joseph Lortz had proposed through his research into the origin of the Reformation, that "the Reformation is a Catholic concern; that Catholics had a share in the cause and also share in the guilt . . . We must take our guilt upon ourselves".[14] And we are summoned to bring back "the riches of Luther into the Catholic Church". [15]

IV

NEW PROBLEMS

Research on Luther in recent years—Catholic as well as Evangelical (the "fronts" are no longer identical with confessional boundaries)—focuses more and more on the young Luther. The questions of Luther's radical change, the time of its occurrence and the extent of the reform have not yet been abandoned. The discussion also takes in the question of what was new and what Catholic in Luther's exegetical lectures between the years 1513 and 1518. From the point of view of the history of theology, there would appear to be agreement that Luther was strongly influenced by Nominalist theology and that he even described himself as an Ockhamist. But he was at the same time turning sharply against this theology, rejecting it as alien to the Bible, hair-splitting and Pelagian, and he was seeking to bring about a return to Augustine.[16]

My demonstration that Luther did not nail the 95 theses on

[14] *Die Reformation als religiöses Anliegen heute. Vier Vorträge im Dienste der Una Sancta* (Trier, 1948), p. 104.

[15] J. Lortz, "Martin Luther. Grundzüge seiner geistigen Struktur," in *Reformata Reformanda* (Festgabe für H. Jedin, I, edited by E. Iserloh and K. Repgen, Münster, 1965), p. 216.

[16] Cf. E. Iserloh, "Sacramentum et exemplum. Ein augustinisches Thema lutherischer Theologie," *ibid.*, pp. 247-64.

indulgences on the door of the Schlosskirche in Wittenberg, but that he sent them, on October 31, 1517, to his Ordinary, the Auxiliary Bishop of Brandenburg, and to the Deputy for Indulgences, Archbishop Albrecht of Magdeburg-Mainz, and that he only published the theses after these bishops failed to react, has caused some stir in Evangelical circles.[17] Moreover, if this —the nailing of the 95 theses to the door—actually did not take place, then it becomes even clearer that Luther did not boldly break with the Church, but that unintentionally he "became" a reformer. Of course, this lays an even greater responsibility on the shoulders of the authorized bishop. For Luther had allowed the bishop time to react out of his own pastoral concern for souls. He was in deadly earnest in his petition to the archbishop to remove the cause of scandal before great shame fell upon him and the Church. Moreover, there was a good chance of using Luther's challenge, which led to a break with the Church, to lead to her reform.

Further agreement is to be found in the fact that Luther as an existential thinker made especially meaningful the personal demands of the Christian message; he did not speculate on the truth at a distance, but as a seeker and a struggler, he sought to grapple with it and to reach its inner fullness; theology is for him a *disciplina experimentalis, non doctrinalis* (WA 9, 98, 21).

The facts of salvation are for Luther at all times the past reaching into the present. They take on their full meaning when they work themselves out in the Christian and become actual in his spiritual faith. Of what value is it that Christ has shed his blood for the forgiveness of sins, if he has not died "for me", not shed his blood for the forgiveness of my sins? This "pro nobis" significance of the death and resurrection of Christ brings Luther to the expression in which he shows us Christ as a sacrament for us. This Christ-event has not reached its conclusion in itself, but it is a sign, *i.e.,* it points beyond to the salvation-event in man, and also brings about that salvation-event in him. "Every word, every event of the Gospel is a sacrament, *i.e.,* a holy sign through

---

[17] *Luthers Thesenanschlag, Tatsache oder Legende?* (Wiesbaden, 1962).

which God works in the believer that which the event signifies." [18]

This contemporaneity with Christ makes possible the tropological interpretation of the psalms as Luther—and Augustine —used them. In this way, what in its literal meaning is valid for Christ can be affirmed of Christians. But to call this "existential interpretation", as Gerhard Ebeling and in connection with him the Catholic Albert Brandenburg[19] does, is false, if thereby the actuality of the salvation-event in Luther is called in question, or is considered to be minimal for Luther.[20] The fact of redemption does not come to pass in the Word. But the Word, like the sacrament, is the *vehiculum* by means of which the salvation-event comes to the believer and is applied to him. The task of Catholic research in the question of Luther will be—in the coming period, in view of a one-sided emphasis on the theology of the Word in the case of Luther—to bring to the fore the significance of the sacrament in Luther's writings, and to demonstrate, against an existential evaluation of Luther, the significance of the objectivity of the fact of salvation for him, for, if it was ever true for anyone, then it was certainly true for Luther: "If Christ is not truly risen from the dead, then is our faith vain" (1 Cor. 15, 14).

[18] WA 9, 440; for further treatment, see E. Iserloh, *op. cit., passim.*

[19] A. Brandenburg, *Gericht und Evangelium. Zur Worttheologie in Luthers erster Psalmenvorlesung* (Paderborn, 1960); cf. on this matter E. Iserloh, " 'Existentiale Interpretation' in Luthers erster Psalmenvorlesung," in *Theologische Revue* 59 (1963), pp. 73-84.

[20] Cf. A. Brandenburg, *op. cit.,* pp. 139f.: "Here it is evident that a fact in the salvation-event, the ascension, which is also an historical event . . . is not only represented cognitively, but *first begins to exist as a reality* in knowledge." "What the kerygma is for Bultmann, so is more or less the judgment-Word and the Gospel-Word for Luther. . . . For Luther the Word is something of the present, not in the sense of an *anamnesis* or a *repraesentatio* of a salvific fact which, though fulfilled in itself, is called back to the present by the Word. No, the fact of redemption takes place first of all in the Word itself" (p. 150). Very recently, A. Brandenburg has emphasized: "We are not seriously thinking of making an existential thinker out of Luther." Cf. "Auf dem Wege zu einem ökumenischen Lutherverständnis," in *Reformata Reformanda,* I, pp. 313-29.

Ernst Wolf/*Göttingen, W. Germany*

What Did Luther Actually Intend?

I

LUTHER'S GRADUAL THEOLOGICAL DEVELOPMENT

Scholars who dealt with Luther used to put the decisive break-through of his awareness of being a reformer, his experience in the "tower", as early as possible, although today they show more reserve. However, it should not be overlooked that Luther himself had a curiously negative attitude toward his early writings and addresses in which he thought he had been too easy on the pope, *i.e.,* on the institution and doctrine the pope represented. It is not until the second lecture course on the psalms in 1519 that his judgment changed.

This does not necessarily contradict the statement that his gradual *theological growth* had started earlier. This growth began with the loosening of "the authority and authorities of Scholastic theology against which he used the strongest terms, although he was clearly not in the least aware of the fact that, by doing so, he was dissociating himself from the presuppositions of Catholic theology and the Church at large of that period. His devotion to this Church remained wholly intact until 1518 when he criticized particular abuses in a lively, blunt and often passionate manner. He believed that his practical attitude and theological ideas were wholly compatible with those of the Church: it was only a matter of shaking up her proper authorities in order to have these abuses

16

eliminated or at least mended. Even when he had already broken with certain elements of piety in the Church, insofar as he himself was concerned, he still practiced them quite ingenuously. . . . He fulfilled his ecclesiastical function most seriously, just as he continued to observe his monastic duties in all seriousness until a late date" (Aland).

All this was accompanied in Luther's own spiritual life by spiritual conflicts centered around the problem of penance and worry about predestination. These conflicts gave the "existential" character to his theology, for he tried to tackle them by having recourse to Scripture, and this made it possible to lift the personal experience onto the level of a generally valid theological awareness. This—as Luther always maintained—happened first in the question about indulgences, which helped him to put the problems and the attempts at solution into a new perspective. But not until his meeting with Cajetan in Augsburg and the disputation of Leipzig did it become clear to him that he was in theological conflict with the Church of Rome and her teaching. The result of the debate of Leipzig led to:

1. The clarification of his *"Scripture principle":* the exclusive authority of Holy Scripture and the self-interpretation of Scripture in the light of its witness to Christ.

2. His demand for a *spiritual concept of the Church* as a result of his earlier perceptions, but without abandoning the visible Catholic Church and his claim to belong to this Church: the Church as *creatura Verbi,* the creature of the Word; the community of persons under Christ as Head; the general priesthood of the faithful as opposed to the exclusive claim of the hierarchy and the papacy to the power of the keys and the interpretation of Scripture; the functional organization of the Church as a human institution, based on Romans 13 instead of Matthew 16; the refusal to accept the papal ban.

3. The gradual discovery of the *papacy as Antichrist* in the sense of the demonic situation of a Church which forces both the word and man's conscience.

4. Together with all this, the emergence and positive ac-

ceptance of the question of a *reform of Christianity* and the search for ways and means of achieving this.

What Luther, therefore, *really* wanted may perhaps be seen in how this development and the main questions of his theological achievement are held together: a critical unfolding and application of what is contained in the confession of the *Kyrios*—the statement that Christ alone is "my Lord"—and this in the context of the problem about the true Church and the membership of this Church. This is what I would like to explain in what follows.

II

CHRIST ALONE IS THE LORD

The Gospel is the criterion of all religion. This was Luther's reply to the question about the nature of the Gospel, and about the relation between Gospel and religion, whether Christian or non-Christian. This reply includes Luther's work as a reformer. All attempts to explain Luther's concern by approaching it from the point of view of one's own theological ideas and to understand it accordingly are inadequate compared with what he himself once described as the sum of all his endeavor: he sought nothing "except that Holy Scripture and divine truth should come to light" (WA 38, p. 134).[1] That was at the same time his motto: *nihil nisi Christus praedicandus* (nothing is to be preached but Christ).

[1] In view of the vast literature on Luther, reference is only made to the works actually quoted and some special studies which provide a more extensive foundation for the arguments set out here. A selective bibliography may be found in "Luther" and "Lutherforschung" by E. Wolf in the *Evangelische Kirchenlexikon* II (Göttingen, 1958) and in "Luther," by H. Bornkamm, and "Luther II," by G. Ebeling, in *Die Religion in Geschichte und Gegenwart* IV (Tübingen, 1960).
Abbreviations: WA = *D. Martin Luthers Werke,* complete critical edition (Weimar, 1883 to date, 99 volumes); BSLK = *Die Bekenntnisschrift der Evangelisch-Lutherischen Kirche,* critical edition 1930 (5 ed.), 1964. For the present state of research, see *Lutherforschung heute. Referate und Berichte des 1. Internationalen Lutherforschungskongresses Aarhus 1956,* ed. V. Vajta (Berlin, 1958); K. Aland, "Der Weg zur Reformation," in *Theol. Existenz heute,* New Series 123 (Munich, 1965), p. 109.

The idea that Luther's teaching on justification is the formula expressing his reformatory confession of Christ not only corresponds to the birth of Luther's teaching on justification but also helps us to see the foundation of his theology in an expansion of the early Church's christology. In his "creative reproduction", he made "the dogma of Christ in the early Church the basis of all theology" (W. Maurer), so that one might see in the *simul* of *iustus simul et peccator* (righteous and sinful simultaneously) an interpretation of the early Church teaching about the hypostatic union. This thesis undoubtedly goes too far if it means to be exclusively valid even for the first stages of Luther's theology, but the christology of his first lectures on the psalms (1513-15) and its close links with an ecclesiology based on the body of Christ rule out undeniably any attempt to derive Luther's theology simply from a tie-up of Scripture and conscience. The ecumenical character of Luther's thought and his grasping at the traditions of the early Church helped to shape his decisive question about the true Church, and his teaching on justification aimed precisely at finding a judicious answer to this question. The belief in Christ as present in the Christ that is preached, and not the *doctrine* of justification, was therefore the framework of his interpretation of Scripture. And so he concentrated on regaining and securing the confession, *Jesus Christ is my Lord*. This means: on the concrete expansion of this confession of the *Kyrios*. This is also the final answer to Luther's question, so often misunderstood, about God being merciful to him.

The Reformation, then, was for Luther nothing else than the permanent return of the Church to her mission of preaching, understood ecumenically and universally as a constant self-critical examination of how closely she is in fact bound to the message of the Gospel. The revolutionary element in Luther's Reformation —the word "Reformation" plays but a very small part in his work—thrives on the revolutionary element of the Gospel itself. And so Luther, according to his own judgment of himself, was, against his will, valued at first as a prophet and not explicitly as a reformer until the end of the 17th century.

When Luther repeatedly stated, almost as a formula, that his work brought something *new,* this can only mean that he achieved not two (*Articles of Schmalkalden,* BSLK 411, 20; WATr 4, 4172) but three things: apart from the regaining of the pure preaching of the Gospel and the administration of the sacraments according to the Gospel (which includes the reduction of their number to baptism and the eucharist), there was a third achievement, not less important and corresponding to the first two, namely, *the new attitude toward human existence in the communal life of society on earth,* setting man free for his earthly vocation.

Christian life no longer was for him what it so commonly was in the Middle Ages and still partly is in pietism and modern Protestantism, namely, a mainly "private" concern or a matter of living in an ecclesiastical environment in rejection of the "world" or with a reserved attitude toward this world. The whole Scripture, says Luther, shows "that there never was a saint who was not concerned with politics or economics" (cf. WA 40, III, 207). The Christian has no such thing as a "private" existence. This discovery, with its effect on society and linked with its declericalization, meant that the world is again believed in as created by God, as the place where the faith is confirmed in obedience and imitation, as the proper place for *sanctification,* as the field in which the freedom of a Christian operates, and all this without proclaiming a "Christian society" or a "Christian State", however often one may address a "Christian authority".

The order of the kingdom of God and the ordering of the world remain two different things. The Church is neither the law nor the ideal of society, and she has no dominion over society. World and society as the place for sanctification means that faith urges man to obey, to bear witness to Jesus Christ before the world and to practice love toward his neighbor. In his treatise on Christian liberty Luther expressed this very boldly: the faith urges man to become a Christ for the other, just as Christ meets me and is met by me in his saving love (cf. WA 7, 66). Sanctification, therefore, is no longer a man's concern with his own justification and beatitude with the help of pious exercises and moral perfection. Sanctification rather has the experience of justification as its enabling presupposition and earthly life, in solidarity with the needs of this world, as its preexisting condition. Just as God, in one of Luther's descriptions, put Adam in the Garden of Eden with the mandate to subject the earth to himself (cf. WA 7, 61), so is the Christian again directed toward the world. He will bear witness to God's salvation by active selfless service in order to overcome that lack of salvation of this world which fell into disorder through man's turning away from God. Alluding to a phrase of St. Augustine, Luther said that through one man original sin entered into this world (WA 56, 310, 3), and man could only see this through Christ's revelation and become aware of it in the admission of his sinfulness before God. Thus, the Christian, delivered and called in faith, exercises dominion over the earth as God's collaborator (cf. WA 40, I, 436f.) in the reconciliation of the world with God. This takes place in the framework of an encounter between the kingdom of Christ and the kingdom of the world, of Gospel and law, under God as the leader in both spheres.

For Luther, this faith in Christ was centered in the fact that one trusts in the granting of the forgiveness of sins proclaimed in the Church, for only such a faith is full recognition of Christ's lordship in its absolute freedom and exclusiveness. But man constantly withdraws from this for the sake of his own supposed freedom and self-assertion. In his commentary on St. Paul's Epistle to the Romans, Luther expressed this once as follows: "We believe God that we must be justified, but we try to achieve this by ourselves in our praying, wailing and confessing; yet we do not want Christ because God can give us his justice without Christ." At least, that is what we say. To this Luther replied with reference to Romans 3, 22; "God does not and cannot want this. . . . Justice is not given except through faith in Jesus Christ. . . . This is the way it suits God and nothing can be changed in this" (WA 56, 255). Not to seek salvation through Christ is arrogance and presumption. Thus, *faith in*

Christ and justification and forgiveness of sins coincide. In taking up the sinner's cause, in humiliating himself for him, in interceding for him, in identifying himself with him and rescuing him from the power of sin and death, from the dominion of the devil, and so freeing man from his selfishness, and also in religious matters—it is in all this that Christ shows himself as the "Lord of life". Everything rests on this "article" of faith in Christ: "And where this article begins to totter we are lost" (WA 47, 541). "So all turns on this article about Christ and all depends on it. Whoever has this has everything" (WA 46, 19). "This article and no other makes one a Christian (WA 33, 160). According to the articles of Schmalkalden of 1537, this is the "main article where one can neither abandon nor yield anything, even if heaven and earth fall down or whatever will not remain. . . . And it is on this article, on which everything is based, that we teach and practice against pope, devil and world . . ." (BSLK 415f.).

In line with this proclamation of Christ, in which Christ is preached as "my Lord" because of the forgiveness of sins, and at the establishment of the Reformation in the electorate of Saxony, the parish priests who had been taken over were admonished in the articles of visitation (1527-8) to link *all* the preceding articles of faith in the Apostles' Creed to the remission of sins (cf. *Corp. Reformatorum* 26, 12). The pure preaching of the Gospel is therefore the preaching of the lordship of Christ because of the fullness of redemption which Christ established with the forgiveness of sins. This point determined Luther's understanding of theology, his view of the Church and his idea of the Reformation at large.

III

CRITICAL DEVELOPMENT OF THIS CONFESSION OF CHRIST

1. *Understanding Theology*

For Luther the object of theology was not God in his essence and attributes as the principle and end according to which the rest of theology is usually organized in detail. Rather, as Luther himself put it: "The proper subject (*i.e.,* object) of theology is man, guilty and lost, and the justifying God and Savior. What is sought beyond this is but error and futility in theology" (WA 40, II, 327). Theology does not begin with the ground of being, but precisely there where Adam made himself "Lord and possessor", aware of his self and his power, and thus putting himself into a sinful condition toward God and man within the history of God's dealings with man. This is, therefore, the object of theology insofar as both are only known in their true reality through the Word of revelation. The object of theology, therefore, corresponds to the contents of the Word of God, and thus only to him who, as the pledge of forgiveness of sins, of the resurrection of the body and eternal life, is the Gospel. The object of theology and the basic theological axiom coincide in the acceptance of the first commandment, the "whole of the Gospel". The basic theme of justification and that of theology are really identical: the divinity of God (*Gottes Gottsein*).

2. Luther's View of the Church

As a consequence of what has been said, the *Church,* too, is seen as a factor of the revelation: "The Church is hidden, the saints are withdrawn" (WA 18, 652; cf. 51, 508), as a "submissive sinner before God till the last day", that is, "only holy in Christ, her Savior" (WA 38, 216), as the "creature of the Gospel" of whom it is said: "The whole life and substance of the Church is in the Word of God" (WA 7, 721). The Church, too, is inserted into the happening of the Word, not in a kind of spiritualized way but ordained toward the reality of the Word in the person of Christ, which reality carries the Church. In opposing the traditional four "marks" or "notes" that signify and constitute the Church (based on the Nicene creed)—unity, sanctity, catholicity and apostolicity—Luther said in controversy: "The one eternal and infallible note of the Church has always been the Word" (WA 25, 97). This is the most pungent expression of his view of the Church, and the equation of the "live voice of the Gospel", "Christ's kingdom" and the "Church" is characteristic of this view. The Church is the Church of *Christ* in the strict sense. He is the Head and he alone remains her sole Lord.

It is true that one cannot derive Luther's view of the Church exclusively from his teaching on justification, but there are close links. This becomes clear in the question about the nature of the Church's unity. This unity should not be understood as organic or as an organization, but strictly as a spiritual unity. This is not an "outward or legal unity", "deliberately put together" and "intentionally established", nor is it a "worldly convention": it is "Christ in me and truly one body with us" (WA 33, 235), "one thing" (WA 46, 713). The "one" of John 17 refers to the exclusive, hidden unity given in Christ in all outward appearance which corresponds to every justification of God given in the experience of justification. Just as the Son alone is the "image of the invisible essence of God" and the Christian is the *"outward* and not internal resemblance and image of God" on the basis of the "alien justice" promised to him, so does this apply to the mystical body of Christ: "Thus we are in the Church one body of Christ, but *outwardly* and not by nature" (WA 39, II, 298A). This, however, can only be *in faith* because the Church shares in Christ's appearance of a servant. The body of Christ exists in the state of "becoming" and in "coming", in hiddenness and conflict. This one and true Church of Christ meant everything for Luther. He claimed in the strongest possible manner to be "in and of" the true Church of Christ, in continuity with the early Church, and even within the early Church herself.

3. *His Understanding of the Reformation*

In his own judgment Luther was not an "innovator". The Reformation was for him not a "renewal of the Church in head and members" as a reform of the institutional form of the Church. It did not establish a "new order", but was explicitly the apostolic Catholic Church reminded of her sole reason for existence, of her nature as "creature of the Word", and so of the Word itself as the basis of self-criticism. One should not forget that the 16th-century Reformation did not happen in an age of religious deso-lation, of a declining, tired and dying piety, but precisely in an age of intense and even excessive religious practice, pious activ-ity and religious agitation. It was exactly this enhanced religious life in the Church, this intensification and expansion of cultural and pastoral activity, that constituted the "innovation" against which Luther's Reformation turned. But then, this Reformation itself was accused of being an "innovation". Yet, it was in no sense an "offensive" but a deliberately "defensive" operation in the contemporary history of the Church. In the great theological controversy about the question: "What is the true Church?", Luther in 1541 defended the "old" Church as the true one against the false and depraved Church of the papacy along these lines in his book *Against Hans Worst*. It dealt with the factual question that the papists "allege that we have fallen away from holy Church and have set up another, new Church" (WA 51, 476). In the schema of the "two kinds of Church from the world on till the end" (*von der Welt an bis zu Ende*) he argued in de-tail, following St. Augustine, "that we have remained in line with the true Church of old, in fact, that we are the true Church of old, while you have deserted us, that is, the old Church, and have set up a new Church over against the old one" (*ibid., 478*).

In doing this, Luther did not give a complete list of the "in-novations" but concentrated on the great "innovation" of putting aside the one element by which the Church lives as Church, *the Word of God*, and it was on this basis that he distinguished "new" from "old". Consequently, what was "new" was understood on this basic principle as an "addition" to the Word. He used this basic category to criticize natural religion as much as the existing piety and the nature of the papacy, and he interpreted this as "satanology". Just as man obstructs God's saving deed by adding "I" to everything, so does the papacy obstruct the Word of God by adding its precepts and laws. This addition is in both cases the work of the "one who adds". This is the real name of the devil and this is "in Hebrew, *Leviathan*, that is, one who adds, who makes more of something than it can be. And so, all those who add human law to God's law are decidedly the enemies of God and the apostles of Leviathan, and whoever accepts and holds on to them is the disciple of Leviathan" (WA 8, 141).

The Reformation differs from all this in that "we bring in nothing new and add nothing" (WA 51, 482). But insofar as the teaching on justification was the central and comprehensive formulation of the new proclamation of Christ, purified of all "addition", and constituted the answer of the Reformation to the central issue of the true Church, the "renewal" of the Church was rooted for the reformers in their theologically legitimate concept of *metanoia, i.e.,* penance. Luther could only take up the formula, "the Church must always be reformed", in this sense, and in no way as an elaborate program of reform.

Jean Bosc/ *Paris, France*

What Would Calvin Say to Present-Day Catholics?

I s this question somewhat anachronistic? First of all, is it possible to see Calvin today as he would wish to be seen? For Catholics, as well as for the vast majority of Protestants, the French reformer will appear, with Luther, Zwingli and a few others, to be one of the Fathers of Protestantism. Thus, one is always tempted to consider him in the light of the whole subsequent evolution, and to look on him as a theologian who established the doctrinal lines of the Churches of the Reformation. But is this not to distort the image of a man who did not wish to be the founder of a new Church, but rather the reformer of the Catholic Church of the West, and who never ceased to lay claim to the authentic tradition of the Christian Church? Nor did he look upon his teaching as a completed accomplishment, but as a teaching stemming in every sense from the judgment of the Word of God. What he said of the Fathers of the Church—namely, that if they had written wisely and well of many matters, "in some matters it befell them, as it befalls all men, to err and to be mistaken" [1]—he applied to himself as well. It is not so easy today—and it is no easier for Protestants than it is for Catholics—to discern the real intention and to uncover the real profile of this man.

On the other hand, is not the situation of Catholicism today

---

[1] *Institutes of the Christian Religion* (Paris, 1957), I, "Epistle to the King," 36; (German Edition of O. Weber).

profoundly different from what it must have been in the 16th century? The Roman Church was then living in a "triumphalism" from which she wishes to free herself today. Many of the deformations that marked her then have disappeared, or (at least to a certain degree) have been arrested or stamped out. She wishes to become openly maternal rather than imperial. And even on the doctrinal plane, has she not recently restored the balance which, without bringing her to deny her traditional teaching, might be considered to be the answer to certain of the requests put forward by the reformers? Within the Church, have we not assisted at an impressive biblical renewal? And even in the area of the doctrine on justification and sanctification, which was at the origin of the Reformation "explosion", are we not agreed today that there is an extensive area of consensus among Catholic theologians and the reformers? Hence, can we not say that the appeals for reform have been answered and question whether Calvin still has something to say to Catholics today?

And yet, it would be an error, and not simply a hypothetical one, to think that the matter is settled. If we are ready to listen to Calvin, not as a protesting schismatic or as the proponent of a system which must be taken or left, but as a Christian teacher in search of the Church's faith, I believe that his fundamental requests remain so many burning actualities. I shall here concentrate on three principal ones.

I

Unconditional Submission to the Word

The first is his appeal for an unconditional surrender or submission to the Word of God as it is attested to and published in Sacred Scripture. In all things the Bible must be for us "guide and mistress". This does not in any sense mean that Calvin held to a narrow and rigid "biblicism". His attention to the voice of tradition was perfect, in particular to the tradition of the first five centuries of the Church's life. He openly recognized that the Church has the duty "to set out in clearer terms the things which are shown to us obscurely in Scripture", but he adds, "provided that what we say serves to express faithfully the truth of Scripture, and that this can be done without too much license and for good reasons".[2] But in any case, the articles of faith, like the preaching of the Church, had to be based on the truth of the Bible.

We are not here speaking of a principle which is invoked or appealed to. The doctrinal work of Calvin is supported by immense exegetical labor, as witness the monumental volume of his commentaries on the Old and New Testaments. The properly dogmatic treatises—and in the first rank among them, the *Institutes of the Christian Religion*—give constant evidence of his concern to found his teaching on Sacred Scripture. An evidence of this is his permanent preoccupation to avoid what he calls "vain speculations", so as to hold fast to the very substance of the Word of God. This call for a rigorous and profound submission to Scripture is an admonition which is significant for present-day Roman Catholicism. It seems, in fact, that in spite of all that has been done—and the success of these efforts is incontestable—there remains a hiatus between the considerable work of the exegetes and doctrinal elaboration properly so-called.

After the second session of Vatican Council II, Oscar Cullmann, studying the place of the Bible in the Council, noted that if several of the schemata had been nourished on an authentic biblical source, there were others which, in spite of many citations from the sacred books, had only a somewhat distant relationship with biblical thought: ". . . . when we look more closely we note," he says, "that very often the numerous biblical references added in parenthesis are not the real basis of the exposition, but that they are only '*dicta probantia*' destined to establish, as an afterthought, a somewhat external relation between the already established text of the schema and the Bible." [3] Certainly, in this area progress had been constant from one session of the Council to the next; the hiatus exists, nonetheless. The

---

[2] *Ibid.*, Chapter XIII/3, 147, 148.
[3] O. Cullmann, "La Bible et le Concile," in *Foi et Vie*, 5 (1964), p. 291.

projected text on religious freedom and the interventions aimed at it showed that still too often in Roman Catholicism a stand is taken on philosophical and anthropological grounds, rather than in the search for a biblical foundation. Moreover, from this point of view all those aspects which have not been the object of the examination of the Council fathers ought to be examined; they, too, should be confronted with the teaching of Scripture.

It is understood that this appeal of Calvin for submission to the Word of God does not mean adhering to all the conclusions to which, in the past, this submission led the reformer himself. To infer this would be to betray Calvin's most profound thought: "This would be to ignore the fact," as Karl Barth writes, "that in decisive circumstances Calvin's words, reasoning and actions represented only in a very imperfect manner his intuitions and intentions." [4] Submission to the Word of God is an "open" attitude which constantly allows this Word to exercise its sovereign power and continually to renew the Church. This is why this attitude is required in the same way today on the part of the Churches of the Reformation as well, and constitutes a fundamental ecumenical meeting ground. Therefore, this appeal of Calvin is, with regard to Roman Catholics, an ever pressing and timely statement.

II

RIGOROUS CHRISTOCENTRISM

A second essential aspect of Calvin's message seems to me to consist in his effort to tend toward a rigorous "christocentrism". Moreover, we are here speaking of one of the guidelines of his theological thought, intimately connected with his attitude of submission to Sacred Scripture. The Bible gives testimony to Jesus Christ who alone is Lord in his union with the Father and the Holy Spirit. To open the Scripture is always to be led toward him; otherwise, we meet nothing but the dead letter. We possess all things in him, and what we might wish to acquire outside him is naught but deceit and illusion. To be sure, here again we may

[4] K. Barth, "Preface to Calvin," in *Textes Choisis* (Paris, 1948), p. 12.

ask whether, in the exposition of his teaching, Calvin was always consistent with this fundamental axiom. But, once again, this is beside the point: attention to Calvin may perfectly well mean to turn aside from particular aspects of his teaching in order the better to follow him in his willed, total respect for the sovereignty of Jesus Christ. In fact, what is here at stake is that Jesus should be recognized as the sole mediator and that he should remain Lord in his Church.

The most important as well as the most violent criticisms addressed to the papacy by the French reformer are regularly based on the certainty that the doctrinal or spiritual aspects he has in mind cast a slur on the integrity and the unicity of the person and the work of Jesus Christ. If Calvin draws up a pitiless list of charges against the Mass, it is because he sees in the re-iteration of this oblation "an intolerable blasphemy against Jesus Christ and the sacrifice which he made for us by his death on the Cross".[5] If he repudiates the intercession of the saints, it is because he sees in it a manner "of attributing now to this one, now to that one, what is proper to God and to Jesus Christ".[6] These examples could be multiplied.

In these matters it is still possible to debate whether, or to what degree, Calvin was unjust in his interpretation of Roman Catholic teaching and practice; we may make allowances and say that abuses of the time should not be confused with the traditional and ordinary teaching of the Church; we may also quarrel with the doctrinal conclusions of the reformer. But his central position seems to me to be profoundly significant and to admit of a question which is never out of date with regard to Roman Catholicism (any more than for the Churches of the Reformation). We may certainly note here that a more and more marked christocentric current is today giving life to theological thinking within the Roman Church; this is true. It remains to ask ourselves whether it is as rigorous and as widespread as Calvin invites us to make it. It cannot be denied that this tendency has shown it-

[5] *Institutes of the Christian Religion*, IV, Chapter XVIII/14, 461.
[6] *Ibid.*, III, Chapter XX/22, 360.

self very vigorous in recent decades in speculation on central dogmatic points: on soteriology, the doctrine of grace and certain aspects of ecclesiology. But can we not ask ourselves whether, even on these points, we have really gone to the end of the line? Above all, are there not very many expressions of doctrine and piety, secondary but nonetheless extremely significant, which require a critical and christocentric examination? In any case, attention to Calvin's teaching would lead us to this.

III

THE INSTITUTION AT THE SERVICE OF THE EVENT

The third aspect of Calvin's teaching which should constitute, I believe, a message from the reformer to present-day Catholics concerns the domain of ecclesiology. This is an area where, in the course of the three centuries since the Reformation, opposition has only increased in stubbornness. Here again it may be said (and not without solid reasons for doing so) that Vatican Council II, on this score, too, has opened up a way through the ice. But has it truly gone to the root of the problem? In modern terms we would say that what Calvin was fighting against when he opposed the papacy was a concept of the Church in which the institution precedes and guarantees the event. In spite of certain ambiguous formulas, he had no quarrel with the necessity for the Church to manifest herself visibly. He knew perfectly well that the Church cannot subsist without form and order, and that these must be those instituted by our Lord Jesus Christ. But the touchstone of the authenticity of this Church, for Calvin, is not to be found in the validity of the institution, but in the living relationship and submission of that Church to the Word.

The Lord Jesus Christ teaches, nourishes, guides and governs his Church by his Word and by his Spirit. To see in the validity of the institution the guarantee of the truth of the Church is to run the risk of the Church's withdrawing from the living Word and setting herself up as autonomous. Precisely this was his concern when he approached the question of the infallibility of the

Church: "When they say that the Church cannot err, this is how they understand it: that so long as she is governed by the Spirit of God, she can go forward confidently without the Word: and no matter how she proceeds, she can feel and speak only what is true: and thus, even should she determine something beyond the Word of God, her pronouncement must be held as a certain oracle coming from heaven. For our part, if we grant that the Church cannot err in matters essential to her life, we do so in the sense that she cannot fail so long as, putting aside her own wisdom, she allows herself to be taught by the Holy Spirit through the Word of God. Therefore, this is the point at issue between us: they attribute authority to the Church outside the Word; we, on the contrary, join Church and Word inseparably to one another." [7]

It is clear that such a text will appear exaggeratedly harsh and unjust to present-day Catholics; they will resent in particular the accusation that the Church has authority without, or outside of, the Word. We know well enough of the attention to this Word so widely manifested at the Council. But even making allowances for the exaggerations that can be attributed either to the situation in the 16th century or to the excessive severity of Calvin, or to both at once, and taking into account the correction of emphasis which will have to be made in this judgment, is not the basic thrust of the problem still with us? Today the question addressed to Catholics would be framed in this way: "Do not the weight of the institution and the authority and the security attached to the institution constitute a threat to the autonomy of the Church? Can the institution truly be at the service of the event?" Moreover, this question, too, touches the Churches of the Reformation in one form or another and in another context.

To sum up: what is at stake in all this—and we find here a permanent theme in Calvin's thought—is the sovereignty and the freedom of God, the sovereignty and freedom of Jesus Christ, the sovereignty and freedom of the Holy Spirit. This reminder is always a timely one for present-day Catholics as for Protestants.

---

[7] *Ibid.*, IV, Chapter VIII, 166.

Alexandre Ganoczy / *Tübingen, W. Germany*

Calvin in Present-Day Catholic Thought

What do present-day Catholics think of Calvin? There is no easy answer. One might be tempted to interpret "present-day Catholics" as those few historians and theologians who have made a special effort to really understand Calvin and his religious thought. But it would be an illusion to think that these learned people exercise a determining influence on Catholics as a whole. Their audience varies, moreover, according to the amount of interest shown in the Reformation in general and in Calvin particularly by different Catholic communities. There is little or no interest in those countries where Protestants, and more especially Calvinists, are in fact not in evidence, either by their numbers, by their historical role or by their conquering dynamism. On the other hand, there is considerable interest in those regions where there is interconfessional tension under any form (*e.g.,* mixed marriages) or where general equanimity or a more advanced attitude allows ecumenical problems to be faced quite serenely.

What is more, one must acknowledge the fact that interest in promoting contacts with Protestants does not always imply equal interest in the person and work of Calvin. Even among the most open-minded Catholics, John Calvin on the whole arouses less sympathy than Martin Luther. His sad, severe and intolerant image and his doctrine of predestination have been so firmly im-

34

pressed on Catholics that even the most enlightened minds have a tendency to pass over him in their ecumenical dialogues. This is easy to do because many Protestants, even those in the Calvinist tradition, seem at times to be ashamed of one of their great reformers. That this is the case was evident last year at the time of Calvin's 4th centenary. Most commemorations to our knowledge were made by historians, theologians or journalists; there were some well-organized expositions, but one rarely had the impression that the name of Calvin, even in Geneva, called forth a lively and cherished presence among most Protestants.

Is Calvin Still a Contemporary Force?

Here certain questions must be raised. Should this be so? Are the history and teachings of Calvin without relevance today? Is not his heritage an obstacle rather than a help in ecumenical dialogue? Would it not be better to ignore him in order to concentrate our efforts on the study of modern Protestant theologians?

To the same degree that distinguished and influential minds in contemporary Protestantism believe themselves obliged to neglect the reformers to the advantage of their modern thinkers, all these questions are answered in the affirmative. For example, the partisans of unilateral "Barthianism" are uninterested in Calvin, unless he is completely "Barthianized". Without maintaining that this is the general attitude among our Reformed brethren, one must still agree that it is rather widespread. The consequence among Catholics is very simple. Those among them who attentively follow present-day Protestantism often let themselves be impressed by what they find most modern in it. Certain people go so far as to be satisfied with the second-hand knowledge that such an attitude presupposes, and they feel no need of studying the 16th-century reformers, particularly Calvin.

Here is where we find the *lacunae* in Catholic ecumenism: too often there is no study in depth either on the historical level or the theological, or, above all, in the most important area, the history of dogma. That is why, in our view, there have been so few good things written about Calvin and his teaching in all of Catholic ecumenical literature.

For our part, we are convinced of the present need among Catholics for Calvinistic studies, and also of the need for going directly to the sources of the Reformation, without which they will never understand Protestantism today.

When one has carefully examined the theological works of Calvin, become acquainted with their sources, extracted their principal ideas, measured their biblical and patristic soundness and appreciated their kerygmatic as well as systematic structure, it is impossible not to recognize the importance of these studies without which most modern Protestant theologians, not only the Reformed but also the Evangelicals, would be scarcely comprehensible. Karl Barth's thought, as he himself recognizes, has its deepest roots in that of Calvin. Rudolf Bultmann, in all that regards the scriptural dialectic of his "existential" theology, is as closely related to Calvin as to Luther. There is without doubt an essential continuity between the great initiators of the 16th-century Reformation and the thinkers of modern Protestantism, a continuity that only a superficial observer can fail to notice. Where there is such a living continuity, it is not right to consider only one isolated stage, even if it is the last and the most present.

For Catholics who are solicitous for the unity of Christ's Church, the *firsthand* study of Calvin has at least as much interest as that of Luther, Mélanchthon, Zwingli, or Bucer. Calvin's eminently and systematically "ecclesial" thought is certainly close to present Catholic ecclesiology. Several essential points of collegiality promulgated at the Council, for instance, seem consonant with the Calvinist teaching on the Church.[1]

Another converging factor is that Calvin attached a greater importance than did any other theologian of the Reformation

---

[1] Cf. A. Ganoczy, "La structure collégiale de l'Eglise chez Calvin et au IIᵉ Concile du Vatican," in *Irénikon* 39 (1965), pp. 6-32; *Calvin und Vatikanum II, Das Problem der Kollegialität* (Wiesbaden, 1965).

to the study of the Fathers of the Church.[2] In a general way one can say that Calvin occupies a central position in the whole history of dogma: it was he who succeeded, thanks of course to his elders, Mélanchthon and Bucer, in giving clear and systematic expression to Luther's theology, while safeguarding, thanks to his training as a jurist and humanist, a considerable number of doctrines and institutions from Catholic tradition.

However, it would be in a way selfish, and it would arouse suspicions of "integrationist" intentions, if our interest in Calvin focused only on his thought where it approximates that of Roman Catholicism. Further study is certainly necessary, and while distinguishing plainly the limits of convergence and the essential divergence, one should not hesitate to learn more from him. It is quite possible, in fact, that *his theology* of the Holy Spirit, what might be called his *christo-pneumato-centrism,* his dynamic conception of the ministry and the sacraments—to mention only a few examples—might have a happily stimulating influence on Catholic theological thought. As for the *history* of Calvin, it could well serve as a lesson to ecclesiastical authorities in any period to find out what methods cause generous souls to revolt and how to avoid making "heretics". If what we affirm here is true, is there any doubt as to the timeliness and usefulness of studying Calvin?

CALVIN MISUNDERSTOOD

Let us suppose now that Catholics, and especially students of theology, in response to arguments such as those given above, want to get to know the French reformer. What works have they at hand?

Within the narrow limits of this article we shall point out, by way of an answer, the results of a test made in a certain number

[2] The definitive edition of the *Institutes* (1559) presents an extremely rich patristic documentation. Augustine, Chrysostom, Gregory the Great, Jerome, Tertullian, Cyprian, Ambrose and Irenaeus are most often cited. Cf. L. Smits, *Saint Augustin dans l'oeuvre de Calvin* (Assen, 1957).

of seminary and scholasticate libraries in France, Calvin's country of origin and the active center of ecumenism. (It seems to us that the situation is probably similar in other countries, with one exception: the Netherlands, where authors like Smits, Lescrauwaet and Alting von Geusau have done much to establish an objective opinion on Calvin.)

The first thing that strikes us forcefully is that no textbook in dogmatic theology in these libraries can be called fair in its treatment of Calvinism. As in the case of the other reformers, the so-called "adversarii", the teaching of Calvin is presented in "quotations out of context" and almost exclusively by way of the condemnations of the Council of Trent.

On the religious history shelf, what do we find? Nothing equivalent to the monographs on Luther by Denifle, Grisar or, especially, Lortz. Only the four volumes on *The Origins of the Reformation* by the very thoughtful Imbert de la Tour, dating from before World War I, give testimony to a solitary effort produced by one lay Catholic historian in order to get out of the ruts of historical polemics. Today this work, in its general tendency as well as its detailed statements, is largely out-of-date in spite of its good qualities. Among actual textbooks of Church history, those of F. Mourret, a Sulpician, and Dom Poulet, a Benedictine, are by far the most important. However, the first author, writing in 1921, presents Calvin "as the embittered son of an excommunicated legist of Noyon",[3] lets us think that he broke with the Church because he was deprived of a canonry,[4] takes up again the accusation of rationalism hurled against Calvin by F. Brunetière,[5] unjustly marks out predestination as the very heart of Calvinist theology and attributes to the reformer "an instinctive horror of any organized Church and all traditional dogmas".[6] As for Dom Poulet, whose history of the Church in 1953 attained its 28th revised and augmented edition, after having developed

---

[3] *A History of the Catholic Church,* Vol. V, pp. 459ff.
[4] *Ibid.*
[5] *Ibid.*
[6] *Ibid.*

Calvin's doctrine of predestination with charm and many quotations out of context, he concludes with emphasis: "There is no middle ground, really: either one binds one's hopes to certitude and hears the voice of the Spirit, or one falls over into the awful abyss of fatal predestination." [7] Emphasizing in turn "bibliocracy", "despotism" and the "sickly irritability" of the reformer,[8] he stigmatizes him as follows: "Calvin is a fanatic: theological pride incarnate, so persuaded of his investiture that his word is always, in big and in little things, divine." [9]

In the libraries we visited, on the same shelf with the history textbooks was *The Church of the Renaissance and Reformation* by Daniel-Rops (1955). Here is the way he summarily judges the reformer: "But Calvin was above all the man who decisively broke away, and for this reason, more than any other, a Catholic can have nothing but horror of him." With "a sort of Luciferlike rigor" he built a wall between the Church of his childhood and the one he wanted "to set up" himself.[10] *Calvin tel qu'il fut* (1955) by L. Cristiani, with a preface by Daniel-Rops, comments on selected quotations from Calvin in much the same perspective. This might have been expected from an author whose opinions on the great spokesmen of the 16th century, Erasmus, for example, are more often than not faulty. Lastly, we mention *Calvin et Loyola* by A. Favre-Dorsaz, a bitterly polemic work which could still in 1951 find a university publisher.

Probably the only attempt at an objective history of Calvin for French-reading Catholics is the work of P. Jourda in *Histoire de l'Eglise* by Fliche and Martin.[11] It is too brief to have extensive documentation and to give precise details, and the use of secondary sources has allowed certain clichés to be handed on (Calvin "founds a new Church", he is a "bitter and complete pessimist

[7] Vol. II, *Temps modernes,* p. 61.

[8] *Ibid.,* pp. 62, 65, 67.

[9] *Ibid.,* p. 66.

[10] *Op. cit.,* p. 489.

[11] Vol. XVI, *La crise religieuse du 16e siècle, Calvin et le Calvinisme,* ch. 1-5.

that nothing can ever sweeten", etc.),[12] yet it has the great merit of resolutely denying polemics and "calumnious legends".[13]

On the encyclopedia shelf there is a sad amount of prejudice in the old ones and a happy openness in the more recent ones. Migne's *Encyclopédie Théologique* (1858) is pleased to mention as probable the "crime of sodomy" of which certain Catholic adversaries of Calvin calumniously accused him.[14] In the *Dictionnaire de Théologie Catholique* (1923) A. Baudrillart begins his article thus: "Calvin, John, head of a religious sect called by his name, Calvinist." [15] He relies particularly on sources that are as unhistorical as Bossuet, Renan and Brunetière; he dwells one-sidedly on the "inquisitorial regime" of Geneva and predestination (5 columns), and he sees in the grandiose Calvinistic effort to "return to the sources" the deed of a "reactionary man". His final word: "He has no other object except to substitute the Church of Calvin for the Church of the pope." [16]

The excellent article of Yves Congar in *Catholicisme* (1949)[17] is principally concerned with doctrine, and is fortunately supplemented by a rather historical article in the *Lexikon für Theologie und Kirche* (1958) by E. W. Zeeden.[18] The article by J. Witte in the *Dictionnaire de Spiritualité* (1961)[19] adds to those rather scarce Catholic writings (along with a certain number of Dutch works, unfortunately not translated) which are entirely objective with regard to Calvin. (We notice that in their bibliographies they refer almost exclusively to Protestant works.) We ourselves were prompted by these same articles to undertake our theological and historical work on the French reformer.[20]

[12] *Ibid.*, pp. 214 and 241.
[13] *Ibid.*, p. 171.
[14] *Dictionnaire du protestantisme*, p. 411.
[15] *Dict. Theol. cath.*, II/2, p. 1377.
[16] *Ibid.*, p. 1395; on predestination: pp. 1406-12.
[17] Vol. II, *Calvin*, pp. 405-21; *Calvinisme*, pp. 421-4.
[18] Vol. II, *Calvin*, pp. 887-91; *Calvinismus*, I, Geschichte, pp. 891-4.
[19] Vol. IV/2, *Le Saint-Esprit dans les Eglises séparées*, Doctrine et spiritualité de Calvin, pp. 1323-7.
[20] Cf. *supra*, note 1. Cf. also *Calvin, théologien de l'Eglise et du ministère* (Unam Sanctam, 48) (Paris, 1964); *Le jeune Calvin, genèse et évolution de sa vocation réformatrice* (Veröffentlichungen des Instituts

PIVOTAL POINTS FOR AN OBJECTIVE JUDGMENT

A summary of the opinions of Calvin found in the books and articles mentioned in the last paragraph would look something like this:

They find in the reformer: "Catholic values", christocentrism, a sense of the visible Church and her universality, an insistence on ecclesiastical authority and the divine institution of the ministry, an awareness of the missionary and social obligations of the People of God and evangelical ethics clearly formulated for all levels of the Christian community. With some reservations of a secondary nature, Catholics persistently reject predestination to damnation and condemn the theandric insufficiency of Calvin's thought as to christology, ecclesiology and the sacraments.

There is an openness toward some of the values peculiar to his theology: its acute awareness of transcendence and the Word of God, its essentially dynamic character derived from its pneumatic and kerygmatic nature, and the prominence it gives to the charisms and to the laity, recognized as the Church in the fullest sense.

One can say that "Catholic opinion" on Calvin is still in gestation. The multitude of books, as venerable as they are outmoded, which four centuries of Counter-Reformation have accumulated, considerably hinder its development according to the requirements of truth. At the moment such an opinion is only expressed by a few specialists who are ahead of their times ("avancés"). In order to bring an end to this anomaly, articles 4, 5, 9 and 10 of the conciliar *Decree on Ecumenism* must be enforced without delay—and everywhere; in other words, let the polemical and false pages of our textbooks be suppressed or replaced, and may a new generation of scholars arise, possessing sufficient courage and enjoying sufficient liberty to study the *sources* of the religious thought of the Reformation.

---

für Europäische Geschichte Mainz, Abteil. Abendländ. Religionsgesch., 40) (Wiesbaden, 1965).

Boniface A. Willems, O.P./*Nijmegen, Netherlands*

Karl Barth's Contribution to the Ecumenical Movement

On May 10 Karl Barth will celebrate his eightieth birthday. No doubt, an uninterrupted stream of good wishes will flow from all parts of the world to Basle, from Catholics and Protestants alike. In Protestant theology his prophetic voice has been heard for a long time. Through his intervention Protestant theology entered upon a new phase in the 1920s. His famous commentary on the Romans turned it from a phase of pronounced "liberalism" toward a new "orthodoxy". As pastor in the small village of Safenwil, Karl Barth, in close contact with his colleague Eduard Thurneysen, had discovered that the "liberal" theology in which he himself had been trained fell short of God's transcendency and of the essence of the faith. The infinite difference between the eternal God and this world should refrain human beings from wanting to approach this God and his works with religious sciences, historical methods and philosophy. All these attempts at liberalism showed, according to Barth, that man no longer really understood that revelation was a *divine* deed. Nor did man sufficiently realize that the act of faith, as a response to this deed, was therefore also a deed of God's Spirit in man by which this man submitted himself to the miracle of an unconditional and unintelligible consent to the mystery of God. As long as man thought that he had to "justify" this "existential" surrender in faith by proving its rationality with the help of all kinds of sciences, he really wronged the essence of the faith. Christianity dwindled into pious ethics.

It is not altogether astonishing that in this tempestuous rediscovery Barth could not work up much sympathy for Catholicism. The emphatic way in which Catholicism stresses the incarnational structure of the work of salvation and the ideas about the analogy of being (*analogia entis*) did not easily fit in with Barth's eschatological vision. Particularly in the field of ecclesiology there was a sharp contrast at first. Still strongly influenced by Kierkegaard, Barth looked upon the Church as an attempt to secularize the transcendent living God. "A Christianity which is not totally and unreservedly an eschatology has, totally and unreservedly, nothing to do with Christ." [1]

In spite of the fact that Barth's original attempt did not seem to offer any opportunity for a large-scale ecumenical confrontation between his theology and that of the Catholic Church, the future proved differently. Quite early, Przywara, Volk and Hamer began a critical investigation of his theses. Above all, the work of Küng, von Balthasar and Henri Bouillard made very many people realize that his theology is most important ecumenically. This interest stretches into two directions: in the field of ecumenical methodology and in the field of theological content. From the *methodological* point of view it has become clear, also through Barth's influence, that one should not confuse genuine ecumenical theology with a vague irenic tendency or with the study of "confessions", *i.e.*, the comparative study of controversial questions in theology. From the point of view of *content*, ecumenical theology was enriched by Barth's basic reverence for the *transcendence of God* (which operates more clearly in various theological treatises than was the case before), by his emphasis on the character of the Church as *service*, and by his *consistently christological approach* (which can also be counted a gain for the method).

[1] Karl Barth, *The Epistle to the Romans*, tr. with a new preface by Edwyn C. Hoskyns (Oxford Univ. Press, London, 1933), p. 314.

I

PROTESTANT SELF-CRITICISM

In order to clarify this rather arid summary, we might mark off some stages in the development of Barth's ecumenical position. In 1928 he read a paper in Bremen, Osnabrück and Düsseldorf on "Roman Catholicism as a Question Addressed to the Protestant Church". Already at this stage we can clearly see Barth's methodological contribution to the ecumenical problem. At the very start of his address Barth began by pointing out that in all our exchanges we so rarely really listen. Too often we sit there *waiting,* ready with our answer, till the other gives *us* a chance to speak. At that moment we seize our opportunity to make our "contribution" to the conversation. Is this really an attempt to answer what the other really said and, still more, what he really meant? Or have we barely listened and is our part in the conversation rather an independent set piece?

Too often the dialogue is but a dual monologue. Barth exhorted his coreligionists to allow Roman Catholicism to put two clear questions to them: whether and how far the Protestant Church is really *Church,* and whether and how far the Protestant Church is really *Protestant.* Through confrontation with Catholicism, Barth felt himself and his coreligionists compelled to examine *themselves.* This method is infinitely more fruitful than any apologetics and any irenicism. One is then compelled to search one's own heart, even if the "adversary" might interpret this as a weakness. In this address, Barth allowed himself the required sallies against Catholicism, but the sharp point of his question was turned again and again to his own coreligionists. Thus he lashed out against the veneration of saints, but at the end his wrath turned on his colleague of Tübingen, Karl Heim, who "did not spurn . . . the introduction of a small litany of all saints, quoting the names of J. S. Bach, Zinzendorf, P. Gerhardt, Tersteegen, Bodelschwingh, Sundar Singh—and we should be grateful that in this context we should at least be spared the name of Bismarck".[2] It was precisely the encounter with Catholicism which Barth seized upon to launch a sharp attack on "liberalism" in his own circle. That is why elsewhere in this address he said: "If I should reach the conviction that the interpretation of the Reformation put forward by the school of Schleiermacher, Ritschl and Troeltsch (and for that matter including Seeberg and Holl) is *right,* in other words, that Luther and Calvin meant precisely *this* in their days, I might not become a Catholic tomorrow, but I would say good-bye to the so-called Evangelical Church. If I had to make a *choice* between these two evils, then, indeed, I would rather become a Catholic." [3]

II

THE DIALOGUE WITH CATHOLIC THEOLOGY

One might call Barth's early opinions about the Church negatively eschatological. He constantly warned in eloquent terms against that overrating of herself to which every Church is constantly inclined. The *eschaton* cannot be anticipated. However, we gradually begin to hear more positive sounds: the Church is called to absolute service, to *diakonia.* On the occasion of the first Assembly of the World Council of Churches in Amsterdam, 1948, Barth fiercely attacked the Catholic Church. We might feel offended at that, but we ought to remember, on the one hand, that the ecumenical climate of those days was still far from pleasant and, on the other, that in all he writes Barth is a really temperamental author. On that occasion he wrote to Daniélou that he was not in the least sorry that the Catholic Church was not represented in Amsterdam. "Your Church could simply not have sat next to us, but (visibly or invisibly) high above us somewhere on a throne. There just is no room for the

[2] Karl Barth, *Die Theologie und die Kirche* (Zollikon-Zürich, no date), pp. 360-1.
    [3] *Ibid.,* pp. 338-9.

rich among the poor. . . . It is asking too much that we should take your claims to superiority completely seriously and at the same time should look forward to your presence among us." [4]

Barth's critical questions sprang from a positive worry. This became very evident during the years that followed. Important theological studies by Catholic authors began to deal systematically with Barth's teaching. Looking back on this period in 1960, Barth observed: "Whatever people may think of me, people cannot deprive me of this honor at least, that since the Reformation not one Protestant theologian has received so much critical, yet positive, and in any case serious, attention at the hands of Catholic theologians as has happened to me now." [5] Somewhat further on he referred to "the well-known book of my friend, Hans Urs von Balthasar, of Basle".[6] He noticed that Catholic criticism of his work managed to balance critical reserve with definite agreement. Alluding to Hans Küng's dissertation on justification,[7] Barth expressed his great surprise at finding there clear proof "that on such a central point as justification there is no essential difference between the teaching of the Reformation as expounded by me and the accurately explained teaching of the Roman Catholic Church". It pleased and astonished him that this book was not only not officially condemned "but was even explicitly accepted by several prominent theologians". Many questions still remain, no doubt, but Barth was glad to recognize the existence of an *avant-garde* in Catholic theology, and with that "there exists for others, and not least for myself, a splendid opportunity, or rather duty, to keep in touch with them".

Meanwhile, several volumes of his main work, *Kirchliche Dogmatik* (Theology of the Church), had already appeared. Here his christological approach became more and more pronounced. The ecumenical significance of this is undeniable but difficult to show

---

[4] *Theologische Existenz Heute,* n. 15, pp. 19f.

[5] K. Barth, "How My Mind Has Changed," in *Evang. Theologie* 20 (1960), pp. 104-5.

[6] H. Urs von Balthasar, *Karl Barth. Darstellung und Deutung seiner Theologie* (Cologne, 1951).

[7] Hans Küng, *Justification* (Nelson, 1964).

in such a brief space. Barth was moved by an intense realization of the *transcendence of God*. To this necessarily corresponds a deeper preoccupation with the central place of *christology*. The great self-revelation of the transcendent God to us took place in the life, death and resurrection of our Lord Jesus Christ. That is why every word about God ("theo-logy") must be marked with this christological sign. This holds also for the theology about creation and in particular about man. Although this logical procedure still provokes many questions, the way he drew attention to this has proved of great importance. Not only did it throw new light on such classical questions as the motive of the incarnation, but, in a much wider context, it affected the character of theology itself. Ecumenical understanding for one another is often still hampered by the difference in theological climate in which Catholic and Protestant scholars work. If Barth's approach is taken seriously, there will be much less danger of slipping into a speculative "theological ontology". In the concrete this may bring about, among other things, that there will be more room for *exegesis and biblical theology* within "speculative" theology. In this way we would show a better response to Vatican Council I when it described one of the important functions of theology as approaching the mystery of God from the connection of the mysteries among themselves and their connection with the ultimate end of man (Denz. 1796).

III

BARTH AND VATICAN COUNCIL II

And so, we return once again to the question of *method* in ecumenism. We have already seen that Barth wanted real questions and problems put to oneself so that one had to reexamine again and again one's *own* position, one's *own* theology. It is his hope that this kind of honest *self*-examination will lead the Christian Churches, at the hour decided by the Spirit, to meet one another at the point of their origin: *in Christ*. The road to-

ward each other does not run along the periphery of the ecumenical horizon, but it is a vertical road, leading down to the
center in depth, where Christ is the beginning and the end, the
eschaton, of us all.

Barth himself has remained loyal to this procedure. Recently,
this became clear in an impressive way when he gave us his
thoughts on Vatican Council II.[8] These thoughts deserve to be
looked at more closely. Barth emphasized that the primary aim of
the Council was a renewal of the Catholic Church. It was not
summoned in order to start negotiations with the Protestants. The
question whether there will be regular contact between the Catholic and Protestant Churches, whether this will be expanded and
even become institutionalized in a certain sense—all this is important, but not the most important. "We others are . . . required to realize that both the convocation and the previous
course of the Council are symptomatic of a certain landslide that
is taking place in the Roman Church, a *spiritual* movement actually taking place there with whose possibility no one had reck-
oned fifty years ago. . . . My question is whether it is not more
important and imperative for us of 'another faith' to direct our
attention and controversy to it, instead of being so formally concerned with future contacts."

With obvious sympathy, he then specifies some points of this
"spiritual movement" that came to the fore in the Council: genuine reverence for Holy Scripture, "surprising interpretations" of
"the relationship between divine and human freedom", of faith
and works, the care for good and industrious preaching and the
reform of the liturgy. He even talks in this connection about "ex-
plosions" within the Roman Church. He believes that "Rome and
the non-Roman Churches are not static power groups". They
are all in movement and directed "toward the unification of all
Christianity as their final end". "The question that confronts
them, first and last . . . is not the cooperation of their different
doctrines and institutions, but this dynamic movement. They are

[8] K. Barth, "Thoughts on the Second Vatican Council," in *The Ecumenical Review* 15 (1963), pp. 357-67.

summoned to give mutual attention to *this* movement. And the present situation could be determined by the fact that for a change we *non-Roman* Christians are in a special way the ones who are *questioned.*"

Barth wonders whether the Reformed Churches have enough flexibility to start and stimulate such a movement in their own ranks. "Do we have any idea . . . what such a fundamental crisis would be and what it could entail? . . . Do we non-Roman theologians not lack too much that interesting and progressive flexibility which characterizes many of our Roman colleagues, interesting because it does not exclude but includes an ultimate responsibility and clear direction?" Barth highly appreciated the courage and Christian vision of the encyclical *Pacem in terris.* What struck him particularly was the clear evidence of an inspired and courageous Christian message. All this leads him to wonder whether prayer for a growing visible unity of the Church of Christ should not be accompanied by the hope of a new pentecostal event in one's *own* Church rather than by the hope of converting the "others".

We should beware, on our side, of misusing this "ecumenical" statement of Barth's. It might lead to an increase of what has already been called the beginning of a new "ecumenical triumphalism". The danger is not imaginary. It is possible to be so ferociously busy at unmasking the old triumphalism in one's own circles that one falls at the same time into a kind of unholy glee at the expense of "the others". This would be so unecumenical as to be unchristian. The only conclusion we can allow ourselves is that we should continue to give a new shape to the message of Christ in our *own* circle. This requires a humble faith, staunch fidelity and a firm hope in the strength of Christ who promised to make all things new (Apoc. 21, 5).

Gotthold Hasenhüttl/*Tübingen, W. Germany*

What Does Bultmann Mean by "Demythologizing"?

The widespread use of the catchword "demythologization" shows that today it is no longer a matter of discussion among scholars but has penetrated into wide circles of the ordinary faithful. In 1941 Rudolf Bultmann used this word for the first time in a thematic way in his essay on the New Testament and mythology[1] in which he set forth his program. His presentation is basic for any discussion of it today.

What did Bultmann aim at with his program? Does demythologization mean an emptying of the faith or a reflection on what is essential in our expression of the faith? Is it a negative and destructive method or is it a positive attempt to make the Good News of the event of salvation that happened once for all more understandable for modern man? The radical attempts of *liberal* theology at demythologizing the Bible cut out, besides all that it considered to be mythical, the proclamation of the Gospel; and so, these liberal thinkers reduced the message of salvation to some eternal and general truths about mankind. In doing so, they destroyed the real truth of the New Testament instead of interpreting it. Rudolf Bultmann wanted to give substance to this interpretation, and for him the task of the present is to interpret the mythology of the New Testament critically, *not* to *eliminate* it.

[1] *Kerygma und Mythos* I (Hamburg, 1954), pp. 15-48.

Interestingly enough, his essay was not intended as an attack on Lutheran orthodoxy or some out-of-date Catholic biblical scholars. Behind it lies Bultmann's attack on the opinions of W. Kamlah who, according to Bultmann, detached the Christian faith from the Word of God and so turned it into a general concept of mankind which would be just as valid without *kerygma* and incarnation. The essay is directed toward those people who have rejected Christianity as a mythical religion and in whose words there is no longer any faith. He wants to bring out the real message. He is concerned with proclaiming the Word of God in the situation of modern man, the man who lives in a world that is vastly different from that of two thousand years ago and for whom this past world no longer has any meaning.

I

DOES SCRIPTURE CONTAIN MYTHS?

First of all, there is the question whether there is such a thing as myth, *i.e.*, a mythological way of speaking, in the Scriptures.

Although the encyclical *Divino afflante Spiritu* (1943) could be seen as an encouragement to tackle the problem of literary genres and of demythologization, Pius XII's encyclical *Humani generis* (1950) was quite clear: "These excerpts from current stories, which are found in the sacred books, must not be put on a level with mere myths, or with legend in general. Myths arise from the untrammeled exercise of the imagination, whereas in our sacred books, even in the Old Testament, a love of truth and a cult of simplicity shine out." The Catholic theologian, A. Anwander, puts the question quite plainly: "Do the 'current stories' exclude the myth? More precisely: can one say that the Bible links up with Babylonian, Persian and other myths without presenting a myth itself? Or should one admit this only for the Old Testament, and not for the New?" [2]

[2] A. Anwander, *Zum Problem des Mythos* (Würzburg, 1964), p. 21.

Today, after fifteen years, Catholic exegetes commonly accept that the representation of the world in the Scriptures must be seen in the perspective of the current mythical presentations of that time. On the very first page of the Bible the presentation of the world links up with that of the time. There are compartments of rain and snow which can be opened; the earth emerges from the water, and the water above the earth is separated from the water underneath it. And while the biblical narrative of creation itself indulges in some powerful "demythologization" by reducing the worshiped and venerated sun to a simple body of light, the overall presentation of the world remains that of antiquity.

Also in the New Testament, the presentation of the world as consisting of three layers is influenced by typical mythical features. This ancient concept of the world, molded by Jewish apocalyptic thought and gnostic myths of redemption, has become alien to modern man. His thought has been trained by the natural sciences. The rain compartments in the sky have become an image of the past that he can no longer accept as true. Technological developments in every field, the discovery of atomic power, space travel—in brief, the way in which modern man experiences and controls the world makes it impossible for him to think any longer of heaven as "up there in space" or of hell as a place "underneath the earth".

Should this throw doubt also on the preaching of God's Word? Bultmann firmly denies this. He demands, however, that we should distinguish between the *form* of the message and the *message itself,* and that this message should therefore be proclaimed in a form which appeals to modern man so that he can see the actual contents of the message. This necessarily implies a distinction which separates the Good News from the form in which it was presented in the past. The mythical imagery found in the Scriptures must be interpreted in a way that corresponds to our present time and space. This means that the Bible must be stripped of its mythical features. Therefore, the point of demythologization is to preach the message of salvation to a mankind that no longer thinks in mythical terms and to preach it in a way that corresponds to his present way of thinking. This is *necessary* if the Bible is still to appeal to modern man and to lead him to a decision taken in genuine faith, not depending on the form but on the message itself. There is hardly a theologian or biblical scholar today who will deny this basic necessity of "demythologization" if he wants to do justice both to the matter itself and to the man to whom salvation must be proclaimed.

However, this positive purpose of demythologization has no intention of making the Bible palatable to modern man at any price, but proceeds from the intentions of the Bible itself. Thus, Bultmann himself says that his purpose is only truly understood when it is realized that "his critical interpretation of the New Testament does not take the present way of thinking as its norm, but the matter itself, so that it is precisely in the critical approach to the matter that the exegete must prove himself faithful".[3] Thus, the basic question in demythologization is "not a matter of translating the Bible into modern language . . . but above all a matter of biblical hermeneutics, *i.e.*, a matter of understanding the true sense of the Bible".[4]

This point is equally obvious when approached from another angle. There are in the Bible opposite statements that cannot be glibly made to agree if we want to do justice to the actual contents of the Bible. For example, while Matthew and Mark report that both robbers reviled Christ on the cross, Luke makes only one refuse the cross of Christ. And even one and the same evangelist has various statements that are not so easy to reconcile. John speaks of Christ being equal to God and at the same time makes Christ say that the Father is greater than himself. And then there is the fact that some books of the Old Testament seem to reject the immortality of the soul, while this immortality is taught in the Maccabees and here and there in the New

[3] *Eine japanische Stimme über die Entmythologisierung Bultmanns* (Hamburg, 1959), p. 7.
[4] *Ibid.*, p. 14.

Testament under the influence of Greek philosophy. P. S. Zedda, S.J.,[5] has pointed out that, in the narrative of the resurrection, two traditions, one from Galilee, the other from Jerusalem, are present which fix the apparitions in such a way that there is no possible chance of making them agree. This factual evidence of the Bible forces us to distinguish between form and the intended truth to be proclaimed and, by the same token, shows the need of a new clarification of the message itself.

II

ARE ALL THE IMAGES USED IN THE BIBLE MYTHICAL?

Proceeding with his analysis of the biblical picture of the world, Bultmann established the fact that the world is not seen simply as the place where natural and everyday things happen. Illness in the Bible is caused by evil powers and forces from outside, and man's death is looked upon as a punishment of God. But happiness and success, too, are brought about by the intervention of friendly powers, namely, God's messengers. The world becomes the stage for supernatural powers, of God and his angels, of Satan and his demons. Apart from this external influence on man, these powers also affect his will and his actions. Good and evil thoughts do not simply rise in the heart of man, but they are inspired by God or the devil. Thus the individual human being is subjected to powers outside his natural sphere, and the same holds for the community and for history. The course of world history is set toward a speedy end, and the cosmic catastrophe is not caused by the planet losing its heat or by a destruction brought about by man's own action, but by the active intervention of forces and powers, and ultimately by God himself who comes as judge of the living and the dead and raises some to life and others to perdition.

In all these statements, which can be multiplied and varied at

[5] P. S. Zedda, S.J., *Chiarificazioni sul Convegno di Padova* (Rome, 1961).

will, we see, according to Bultmann, the *same presentation,* the same image, of the world: *what is not of this world and divine is presented as of this world and human, and what belongs to the beyond is understood as belonging to this present.*[6] This is based on a way of presentation that interprets the unexplained causes, the blank spots on the map of our life, not by unknown *natural* factors but by the intervention of the beyond, an intervention presented in the same way as our own behavior. It is this presentation, this view of the world, which Bultmann calls "mythical", as had already been done by students of the history of religion. It is in this context that we must understand Bultmann's statement that the mythological way of speaking of the Bible is "incredible" in the literal sense for modern man. Why? Because this mythical picture of the world is a thing of the *past.* The preaching of the New Testament had to be in terms of that age. That age is gone, and so is the language which that age in fact used to express itself. But if the mythical picture of the world is gone, the question arises whether the proclamation of the message can still oblige man today to accept this picture of the world. This, says Bultmann, would be meaningless and impossible: "*Meaningless,* because the mythical picture of the world as such has nothing specifically Christian about it, but is simply the world picture of a past age not yet formed by scientific thought. *Impossible,* because the picture we have of the world is not dependent on a decision we take, but is predetermined by man's historical situation." [7]

This situation has changed, and the mythical picture of the world cannot possibly be made real again for modern man. Thus, Bultmann considers that the biblical presentation of Christ's descent into hell and his ascent into heaven can no longer be accepted in this form. This holds also for the mythical presentation of spirits and demons, of miracles, of a mythical eschatology. Lastly, the images used in presenting death as punishment for

---

[6] *Kerygma und Mythos* I, p. 22, n. 2. Bultmann does not consider any other definitions of myth. One wonders how far another definition of myth might lead to another view of biblical facts.

[7] *Ibid.,* pp. 16-7.

sin, the bloody atonement of a divine being, the resurrection of Jesus as historical event, and a world of light into which we enter with a spiritualized (*pneumatisch*) body are mythical images. It must be stressed once again that Bultmann does not mean by this that there are no miracles, that God's Word is not present in the event of Christ, that the resurrection of Jesus is pure hallucination or that death is the end of all, but rather that the *presentation* of the New Testament is a mythical presentation and therefore ineffective for a man who does not think in terms of myths.

One might ask whether it would not be possible to compare the story of the tax money which Peter found in the mouth of a fish with the story of the ring of Polycrates: in other words, to take it as a legend, but to take the cure of the man born blind as historical fact. Bultmann does not accept this position. It is not a matter of picking and choosing; one can only accept or reject the mythical picture of the world as a whole because the manner of presentation affects all the statements of the New Testament. It is impossible here to introduce distinctions and to admit demythologization for one text, for instance, the first chapter of Genesis, and to interpret the story of the second and third chapters in the literal sense, ignoring the mythical presentation. *All the images* in the New Testament are therefore mythical. Bultmann admits that the mythical features are not everywhere equally prominent, and the question we have to solve is how far the expression is influenced by the mythical world picture. Because Bultmann defines myth in the manner expressed above, this notion of myth is, for him, valid throughout.

Is then, according to Bultmann, the whole New Testament all the same a myth? This is the ultimate consequence of Bultmann's theology according to F. Buri in his essay on "Entmythologisierung oder Enkerygmatisierung der Theologie" (theology without myth or without kerygma), written in 1951.[8] Buri, like the liberal theologians, reduces the event of Christ to a general notion of humanity. But Bultmann definitely rejects Buri's ex-

---

[8] *Kerygma und Mythos* II (Hamburg, 1952), pp. 85-101.

planation. If preaching or the proclamation is the presence of the Word of God, the basic question arises whether the *Word* of God itself is a myth and wholly evaporates in symbolism. But Bultmann makes a distinction of quality between the actual speaking of a word and its contents. The factual happening can, precisely, not be reduced to content, symbol or idea. In Buri's theology, without kerygma this happening, God's deed, becomes a general possibility and so loses its historical character. Buri here follows Jaspers who really rejects the whole question of demythologization. He throws out the baby with the bath water and overlooks the essential distinction between the image of the presentation and the reality it signifies. Bultmann, on the other hand, considers that it is only in the process of demythologization that the real purpose of the myth is laid bare, namely, the address and claim (*Anspruch und Anrede*) to be the revelation of a truth which summons man and puts him before a decision. Bultmann admits that the word always has a content, but for him the decisive element is the speaking of this word, and this is address, summons and revelation. But this fact, the event of the word, does not belong to the world picture, but is a factual accomplishment. It is *not* myth.

III

WHAT IS THE CRITERION FOR THIS DEMYTHOLOGIZING?

Bultmann's disassociation from any undoing of the kerygma leaves us with the burning question about the *criterion* for the process of demythologization: How do we decide whether a given statement is part of the world picture or of the intended truth?

The criterion by which we separate the world picture from the kerygma is, according to Bultmann, the possible relevance to *man's existence*. A theological statement is not mythical if it is at the same time an anthropological statement. This criterion is rooted in the encounter with God's Word and with man, and, therefore, in the truth of the *incarnation*. Ever since this action of God, says Karl Rahner, every theological statement has become at the same time an anthropological statement. And with this criterion neither man and his possibilities nor, for that matter, an abstract idea of God becomes the measure, but the relationship between God and man. Whatever does not fit into this relationship and, therefore, cannot have the character of an encounter cannot be the revelation of the Word of God and, therefore, does not belong to the proclamation. All statements which arise from a realization of this encounter and are strictly related to it are *analogous* statements which leave the myth behind as a symbol, although it retains its validity. Thus, the ultimate criterion of demythologization to which the exegete can refer in the measure of his ability is the interplay of theology and anthropology. How far this may turn theology into anthropology, or vice versa, and how far one of these poles can be eliminated are questions which contemporary theology still debates and which at the same time constantly test the validity of this criterion.

In conclusion, we may ask whether Bultmann's explanation of demythologization is too radical or not radical enough.

He will be considered *too radical* by those theologians who are unable to see any mythical speech in the whole world-picture of the Bible. Today, the boundary between the mythical image and the truth of faith is in fact by no means explained in every detail, and many concrete questions still wait for an answer. However, others, who are quite willing to cut out a few things but still consider many images not as mythological which Bultmann would take as such, will also find Bultmann too radical.

Bultmann will be considered *not radical enough* by those who, together with the mythological language, throw out the contents of the kerygma and thereby destroy belief in the Word of God. According to Bultmann, there remains a mythical element for those who consider it mythological to speak of God as *acting,* of God's love toward us and of his will to meet us. But it is certain that this is no longer mythology in the old sense of the New Testament because here the mythical world-picture is recognized as a garment. There certainly remains for Bultmann the scandal and the real paradox of the New Testament proclamation which is expressed in the words that "he emptied himself" (Phil. 2, 7) and in the classical expression that "the Word became flesh" (John 1, 14). Just as he in whom God is actively present and through whom he reconciled the world with himself is, in Bultmann's view, a true historical man, so is for him the Word of God not the word of a mysterious oracle but the sober proclamation of the person and destiny of Jesus of Nazareth in its full significance for salvation history. Here the speaking of God's Word is no longer *mythical*, but *analogous*. To speak of God as acting is not speaking in images and symbols, but analogously, since God has truly acted, and his action does not evaporate in a symbol or idea. The "beyond" character of God is no longer turned into something of this world, as in the myth; it is a genuine paradox that God becomes present in history.

The question for Catholic theologians is whether this analogous speech is not also possible there where Bultmann thinks he has to speak of *mythological* language. One may hope that both Catholic and Protestant exegetes will take up the *unsolved questions* in Bultmann's demythologization and that their work will lead to a solution that does justice to the scriptural witness of the faith and makes the Good News more acceptable to modern man.

In any case, Bultmann himself does not want to bring God's Word itself, at least in its eschatological dimension and its ultimate significance for man, into dispute on account of his demythologization; he rather wants to bring modern man closer to the real purpose of the New Testament proclamation, beyond all the imagery of a past age, so that even today the faith in God's Word may come fully alive again. In whatever light his theology may appear, it is certain that Bultmann does not want to *destroy* and to make the proclamation of the Good News of God's love in Christ impossible. He wants to eliminate what in his view is a *false scandal* and to reach a factual interpretation that suits our present age. And so, modern man has to face a genuine decision whether he wants to accept the message of his salvation in the paradox of a genuine and real faith or remain in his state of unbelief.

Hamilcar Alivisatos/*Athens, Greece*

Basic Orthodox Demands on the Roman Church

The title of this article, suggested by the editor of CONCILIUM, seems to me neither very ecumenical nor conducive to the unification of the two Churches. It takes the historical separation almost for granted, as well as its continuation, and it looks at the difficulties from this point of view. That would be a bad start for the future dialogue between these Churches. When one speaks of basic demands of one Church on another, one presupposes that there will be negotiations where the other side makes counterdemands, and this will certainly not lead to a happy conclusion; apart from this, such negotiations would have to deal with overly peripheral issues, subtleties and compromises which ought to be avoided after the bad experience of the past. And so, I would prefer to treat of those basic demands which concern the method and technique of the dialogue that might help to bring about the right atmosphere.

I

The Notion of the Church
as a Basic Question for a Dialogue

In my view, the old thesis of two Churches (Roman Catholic and Greek Catholic or Orthodox) is no longer tenable, especially since the new relationship between the two Churches that was created by Pope John XXIII. We ought, rather, to speak of the two geographical parts of the one Church in East and West. The theory of the *Una Sancta,* developed on the Protestant side since the foundation of the World Council of Churches in accordance with the Protestant concept of the essence of the Church, does not adequately apply to both parts of the one Church, because for these two parts of the Church the *Una Sancta* never ceased to exist visibly in spite of the schism. The awakening, on both sides, of an ecclesial awareness that had deteriorated through the centuries, has resulted in a growing aspiration for an effective world mission of the one Church, a fact which, apart from the elimination of the schism, remains as the great task of both parts of the one Church.

If all this is true, it is hardly possible to continue to speak of demands, particularly "basic demands", of one Church on the other. For either it is a matter of the local sectors of the one Church which stress their peculiar features within the Church that was never uniform but which, as often happened in the old Church, are full of goodwill and readiness to understand and interpret these features in a spirit of a common and sacred interest (and this would wholly correspond to the new ecumenical spirit), or it is a matter of two different Churches, in the usual sense, which assert the privileges they have somehow acquired, but without any hope of reaching an understanding, let alone of achieving unification and communion. The new line taken by Pope Paul VI and the Ecumenical Patriarch Athenagoras I in Jerusalem wholly points to the first solution, and it would be a great pity if this road were barred by the second one.

Between the two parts of the one Church, difficulties can doubtless exist that could lead to a schism through external historical influences, but these could be met by reflecting upon the nature of the Church. And so, the success of the dialogue depends mainly on a just appreciation of the origin and continuation of the schism and the constant effort at righting it, whether according to the negative conception of "non possumus" (we can do no other), which has prevailed up till now, or according to a new and positive recognition of faults committed in the past.

That is why I think only one basic condition is necessary for the dialogue, namely, the cultivation of friendly relations through the creation of a favorable atmosphere. It is indeed necessary to learn to understand the common foundation on which we work and to acquire the certitude that we stand on one and the same foundation that is none other than the one Church, the nature of which both sides understand in the same way. Any dialogue would be futile if one cannot first agree on this view of the nature of the Church. Only when this basis is secure can we make progress and explain and judge the respective differences. In this connection, the Catholic Church, which has developed her teaching on the Church in Vatican Council II, is in a more favorable position than the Orthodox Church, which has promulgated no new teaching on this point and still clings to the old tradition; but even so, and perhaps even because of this, the dialogue could become useful.

Until now, any attempt at a dialogue between the "two Churches" began with a tenacious assertion of one's own position, with the fact of the separation and with the open or concealed intention of winning over the "opponent" on the basis of one's own legitimate claims. As I see it, and as, in my view, Vatican Council II sees it in its mention of meeting "on an equal footing", the dialogue from now on must be taken up on the basis of a desire for the mutual understanding of the unity of both. This starting point would mean complete agreement on the essence and nature of the Church. The conviction that the essence and nature of the Church can only be one and the same justifies the hope that the differences of opinion can be overcome. The possible agreement on the essence of the Church might show right from the start how the whole dialogue has to develop.

Putting it like this rather simply and perhaps naïvely, I may seem to overlook or ignore the great existing difficulties. But I am convinced, first of all, that we cannot get on with the dialogue as long as we do not agree on the question of the essence of the

Church, and, secondly, that once this point is secured, we shall have no serious difficulties in dealing with theology and history. However, the study of the New Testament must be brought to the fore so that it can help to clarify the significance of the earliest Church. With regard to the results of this study of the New Testament, I am optimistic, because the essence of the Church, as attested in the New Testament, is not, and cannot be, equivocal since no one can doubt that the Church exists in order to continue the Lord's work of salvation in the world.

There remains, then, the controversial issue as to whom our Lord has entrusted with authority in this task. However, the light of the New Testament is powerful enough to clarify the difficulties of the Middle Ages and to show the relationship which binds the early Church to that of the Middle Ages and that of the present day. This leads to the road taken by the early Church in this world and which the Church must take now, as our age demands. There can be no doubt that this continuity is the best proof of the unity and indestructibility of the Church throughout the centuries. In saying this, I do not mean to underrate the later development of the Church in both sectors and its historical justification. But I am sure that the study of history and theology will show the way to unification which, for the moment, cannot be other than that of the coexistence of both existing parts in East and West, as it was before the schism. If this happens with goodwill and without falsification, it will strengthen true and lasting union.

Possibly, such a beginning of the dialogue may seem too difficult for many; nevertheless, I am convinced that the basic issue of the Church's essence provides the best start for a dialogue which in this way will lead to a good end.

II

APPLICATIONS

The following three simple examples from the present life of the Church may perhaps best illustrate what I mean.

1. *The Primacy of Rome*

Without attacking in any way the primatial authority based on the position of the apostle Peter, one cannot overlook the fact that the person and absolute authority of Jesus Christ, the founder of the Church, usually left out of consideration in this context, is far greater than that of the apostle Peter who, at the most, is only the founder of the Church of Rome. Moreover, Jesus sanctified Jerusalem with his bodily presence and not Rome. If the basis of the preeminence of a local Church is the authority of its founder, no one will deny that Jerusalem has a far greater claim to this preeminence than Rome. And if one considers the apostle Peter himself, before he went to Rome he labored in quite different localities, such as in Antioch, and founded Churches there that have better claims to priority than Rome.

Nevertheless, the authority of Rome is fully recognized on historical, mainly secular, grounds, and no one in the East thinks of attacking this authority. However, the recognition, at least in principle, of the earlier authority clearly illustrates the further development of the later authority of Rome that no one questions today. But this later authority cannot blot out, at least in theory, the original authority in the visible Church. Pope Paul VI must have felt this during his first visit to Jerusalem in 1964. Nothing could be more instructive for the interpretation of papal authority today.

2. *The Collegiality of the Bishops*

A second example is furnished by the reintroduction of the collegial status of bishops through the decision of Vatican Council II and the pope himself. The nature and manner of this re-form, which brings the "two Churches" closer together, clearly shows that this system existed in its plenitude in the Eastern Church from the beginning, and that from there it can be interpreted for its application to the cultual and administrative life of the Church.

3. Variety within the One Church

The "tolerance and coexistence" of the various united Churches within the Catholic Church, as visualized by Vatican Council II, show the significance of this concept. The local peculiarities of both parts of the Church are their special characteristics and should not be made the subject of basic demands on each other or the condition of unification of the Church. These local peculiarities do not belong to the essence of the Church. Insofar as they do not encroach upon the essence of the Church, they should be willingly recognized. One should proceed in the same way with particular well-known differences such as sacramental rites, the famous "filioque" addition to the Creed and the consideration due to particular sociological factors, as studied in schema 13 of the Council.

There are still two problems which will create great difficulty in the dialogue. The first is the absolutely necessary decontamination of the air in both Churches, air that has been corrupted by a centuries-old process of poisonous intolerance, fanaticism and basic misunderstandings. This is most important because no unification is possible without the consent of the whole People of God.

The second difficulty arises from the teaching of the development of the Church's tradition that leads to the proclamation of new dogmas. As we all know, this has brought innovations that are unknown in the East and appear unjustified to them. These, too, must naturally be tackled with goodwill, but no one can say how we are going to overcome these genuine difficulties.

With all this it should not ever be forgotten that belief in each other's goodwill, genuine Christian reflection, the power of prayer and the guidance of the Holy Spirit, whose grace "heals all weakness and adds what is lacking", will be of the greatest importance for the success of the dialogue. And even when it has led to the desired unification of the Churches, it should never cease as a genuine controlling process in the Church and as a means of avoiding any new schism from the outset.

Paul Evdokimov/*Paris, France*

Fundamental Desires of the Orthodox Church vis à vis the Catholic Church

Every Orthodox Christian very happily witnesses the "renewal" of the Catholic Church, and notes that the texts of Vatican Council II have been drawn up with the art of not "closing any doors" to future dialogue. This renewal concerns Christendom as a whole and appeals to every Church for frank self-criticism, real repentance and *metanoia* in its attitude toward Christians with different traditions. The solidarity of all, the feeling of common responsibility for the destiny of Christianity, the communion experienced in ecumenical encounters—this astonishingly new climate plucks out by the roots all easy pharisaism, all criticism by a "pure" face toward manifold heterodoxies.

Thus, as the title of this brief article suggests, our focus is on "desires", hopes, suggestions, so as to draw the attention of the West to the ancient and venerable tradition once common to both, and which the East has borne through the centuries as its most precious treasure. Obviously, before formulating these "desires", a realistic point of view must be selected in order to avoid all utopianism and to be very clear as to what is possible and what is not possible for the Catholic Church.

The dogmatic essence of Catholicism lays down certain limits to the dimensions of "renewal". In brief, our discussion is not of dogmas as such, but of their new interpretation. In this perspec-

66

tive the "desires" of the Orthodox Church can furnish Catholic theologians with food for thought, a creative reflection, in order to see if it is possible to integrate these desires with new interpretations of their own dogmatic consciousness.

The great lesson of the early councils is self-abandonment to the Holy Spirit. In these councils he drew faithfully upon the dogmatic truths professed by East and West, declaring and preserving that truth through the Fourth Council of Chalcedon, in a synthesis of belief accepted by both and leaving neither party with any wish to separate itself from the other on dogmatic grounds.

I

DESIRE FOR AN ADEQUATE TERMINOLOGY

A preliminary desire has to do with terminology, some rather unfortunate expressions like "separated brethren" or "the Eastern Churches" (in the plural); the latter is inaccurate with regard to the Orthodox Church (in the singular), which is one and undivided. The recent convocations at Rhodes have assembled the autocephalous local Churches into one single communion, the one Orthodox Church. Thus, the *Decree on Ecumenism,* in speaking of the Roman Church in the singular, places her apart precisely in the center, surrounded by a multitude of "Eastern Churches" as her satellites. This position is the result of a certain ecclesiology, but this ecclesiology predetermines the conditions of dialogue and destroys the balance of a dialogue "between equals". Real dialogue means that each party bears witness to the fullest extent of its vision, confesses its faith, but that each party also is ready to listen and to renew, if need be, the defective elements of its own presentation. Such an attitude is only possible if we accept as criterion a value that transcends all historical institutions. Every part of Christendom is called to a fuller, more profound conversion to God's truth. It is a call to surpass the immobility of the academic ecclesiologies and the rigidity of an expression imposed on all men.

For men of the East, the history of the Church presents a permanent transcendence over historical institutions (which are always defective) in the direction of Orthodoxy. Here the term *Church* is identified with *Orthodoxy* in its theandric ethos, in its divine source. The local Church has life only as a function of Orthodoxy present in the eucharistic mystery, in the apostolic deposit of faith, in the experience of its saints; but, in its theological thinking, it manifests only approaches to the ineffable *pleroma* (fullness), which remains radically negative or apophatic.

The man who embraces Orthodoxy, the unique Orthodoxy of "thus did the apostles and the Fathers believe", finds himself *ipso facto* in communion with the historic Orthodox Church. The dialogue must be directed toward the search for that Orthodoxy, common in ancient times to both East and West, so that *together* they may be able to make a precise statement as to its essential elements. Together, both parties will have to return to the sources in the common past, before there was any separation, so as to find one another again, not in an archaic past, but in the living tradition and in a manner that would become the creator of the actual synthesis of everyday Orthodoxy.

It will be understood that in this context the expression "separated brethren" is somewhat surprising. Separated from what? The concern of every Christian must be not to be separated from communion with the truth of God, with Orthodoxy in its theandric sense which rises above every historical institution, every local See momentarily subject to error, as history has demonstrated on many occasions. To the "separated brethren" correspond, and are opposed, the "uniats". But "uniatism", insofar as it is a method, must be excluded from the ecumenical dialogue. The relations between Rome and the Churches of the "Eastern rite" constitute a question which is bound up with its own interior structure. The "uniats" are not on the same side of the "Roman face" which is turned toward the Orthodox Church.

II

Desire for Mutual Acceptance of Divergencies

After these preliminaries, which make definite certain conditions desirable for dialogue, we wish to draw the attention of Catholic theologians to the Eastern viewpoint on the history of the relationship between East and West. Political events at the end of the 5th century isolated the West; Rome and Byzantium found themselves of necessity facing different problems. Local traditions were formed, and theological thinking was carried on, within differing social, intellectual and spiritual climates. Each tradition, as a distinct type, presented an individualization of the unique revelation in terms of its own proper genius: the "filioque" doctrine or even the filial love for the principle of a paternal power, monarchical in type and finding expression in the person of the pope in Rome; the universalist and centralized ecclesiology of the West, *coexisting* with a very different theology of the Holy Spirit and a eucharistic and conciliar ecclesiology in the East. It is even possible to say that history has no record of any period in which the dogmatic harmony of East and West was absolute. The differences came from the accentuation of many aspects of the same *mysterium,* and these, translated into human language, can never be uniform. The central place given in the East to "negative" or "apophatic" theology shows that even dogmatic formulas are only maximal approaches to the unknowable, who forever remains essentially mysterious in his nature, "eternally sought after".

Theological divergencies and different local traditions were in existence before the rupture and did not impede communion between Rome and Constantinople. The rupture broke the bonds of love and inaugurated an officially sealed and reciprocal isolation. Polemic theology will endeavor to justify the separation; in the end the different "theologoumena" will become dogmatized contradictions. But the important fact of the history of the early centuries teaches us that "refusal to receive" one or another local tradition did not automatically bring with it a rupture in the union. Before the separation Rome affirmed its primacy without causing the East to break away. The ecclesiastical self-consciousness of each part of Christendom varied in makeup and coexisted in a certain *modus vivendi*. The two regimes, each one exercising its influence within its own territorial limits, were not at all incompatible with eucharistic communion. In a state of isolation, the dogmatization of the local traditions of a polemical theology, locked up in the ignorance of the other party, took the edge off the very meaning of unity. Happily, the nature of separation, when it concerns the Church, is as mysterious as the nature of unity.

On the other side of the coin of the "mystery of union" is to be found the "mystery of disunion". God penetrates the wall of silence and manifests his real presence in the disunited parts of Christendom. Canonical illegitimacy does not bring with it invalidation of the reality itself; on both sides of the wall are to be found the same body and the same blood of the Savior. This fact brings us to what may be called the negative (apophatic) aspect of unity. Negative (apophatic) theology and hesychastic tradition teach that the more ineffable God is in his nature, the more he can be experienced in his existence, in his burning proximity. In the same way we may say for the moment that the existing unity defies formulas, but in a certain sense it is evident and can be mystically experienced: at the most profound depth of her mystery, at the heart of her life which is Christ, the Church remains one and undivided.

The Church offers the dialectic not of one thing *or* the other, but of one thing *and* the other at the same time, as the Lord has said: "These things should be done, without neglecting the rest. . . ." The synthesis is not speculative but operative, as the Fathers say: "Truth speaks by herself, in silence." If the sacraments are celebrated and if salvation is given through them, the apparent separation loses something of its negative force of exclusion and excommunication. . . . Agreement on the identical essence of the truth requires the review *together* of all the points of difference since the moment of rupture. Above all, it is absolutely necessary to cease thinking and theologizing "against"; the truth of the other side must be understood and properly situated. This is the essential task of dialogue, which might take the form of a "Council of equals".

The history of the early centuries suggests a reference to the ancient attitude of the "non-reception" of a doctrine which remains a local tradition. To recapture the period before the break means to reduce the dogmatic contradictions to the level of simple differences, and for this to "transdogmatize" together to the maximum the traditions formed after the separation.

III

VALUES PROPER TO THE ECCLESIOLOGY OF THE EAST

This is not the place to touch on dogmatic differences as such. The essential point lies elsewhere. The most ardent desire of the East is to see the West ready to penetrate the very soul of the Orthodox Church, to understand from within not her phenomenology or her teaching, but what is to be found at the source of both, the mystagogic spirit animating them and the contemplative and doxological dimension of the dogmas themselves. This is to touch the most intimate aspect of the experience of God lived by his saints; to touch his very mystery which hides him more than it reveals him; to reach the "unspeakable groanings" of the Paraclete and the vision of his light, so as to seize not the always fragmentary points of view, but, as St. Gregory of Nyssa said: "To see with the eyes of the dove."

The West cannot sidestep the historical fact that it was the "pillars" of the still undivided Church—Athanasius, the two Cyrils, the Cappadocians, Maximus the Confessor, and so many others—who forged the dogmatic consciousness and sealed the foundations of Eastern ecclesiology. It is rooted in the principle of the *Sobornost*—the catholicity of the body in its totality. Historically, its *consensus* found the normative form of its expression

in the institution of the council. But even a council has no authority *ex sese,* nor has it the power of immediate infallibility. The
decrees of a "formally ecumenical" council are accepted on the
plane of the economy of discipline and are passed by the body.
They can be accepted or rejected by the totality of the People of
the Church, comprising the episcopate, the clergy and all the faithful. Not the conciliar structure, but the catholicity and collegiality
of all are the notes of the Church; their historical expressions
may vary. This means that through and by different forms of expression the Holy Spirit alone has authority *ex sese,* recognized
and confirmed by the fact that the truth is really received and
lived by the People of God. In the final analysis, it is the whole
body in its theandric nature and by the voice of tradition which
pronounces its judgment *ex cathedra,* but from the invisible and
mysterious "chair" or throne situated beyond every formal and
juridical principle: "Yea, so the apostles and the Fathers believed!" This laying-hold of the truth is sacramental and liturgical
in nature; it transcends the norms of law and every visible and
formal criterion or organ.

The primacy of honor of the Church of Rome was recognized
by the councils. At the same time, this recognition was accompanied by the statement that every bishop is *ex officio* successor to Peter by the same title as the Bishop of Rome. The
geographic localization of the "chairs of the apostles" never was
important in the East. Each local Church, assembled in its bishop
and integrated into the eucharistic community by him, coincides
with all the others, for each one manifests the same fullness of
the Church of God. The only center by divine right is the
heavenly Jerusalem, which manifests itself in every eucharistic
celebration. Every bishop who is in communion with the venerable patriarchal centers of historical Orthodoxy is a bearer of
the Word. The bishop, at the head of the Church whose glorious
past marks her with a preponderant role, is the one who "presides
in love" without any pretension to universal jurisdictional power.
In the East, episcopal power established by divine right is exer-

cised within the diocese and cannot in any way be extended outside and beyond its own diocesan limits. In its eucharistic fullness
every Church has no other center than in its Head, Jesus Christ,
always present, and represented symbolically in the liturgy by the
local bishop who, with his people, makes up the whole, inseparably linked to the Head by the action of the Holy Spirit.

IV

To Rediscover the Role of the Holy Spirit

In order to understand well the foundations of the Eastern
traditions of the conciliar period, we must return to the source of
the Fathers' knowledge of God; this is perhaps the most important point. Easterners are aware of the comparatively small
attention—by comparison with the East—which the West ac-
cords the work of the Holy Spirit as the "second Paraclete", of
the relatively minor importance attached to the event of Pentecost
in the life of the historic Church, to its prophetic charisms, to its
eschatological and parousiac dimensions.

The "signs of the times" have suggested to Paul VI the vision
of "fraternal charity, ingenious in finding new ways of manifesting
itself". This need to be more inventive is an appeal to all the
powers of the new holiness with the love that works miracles.
It postulates and formulates the ecumenical *epiclesis—Veni,
Creator Spiritus*—the unceasing invocation of the ecumenical
Pentecost, for on that day the very essence of the Church has
been shown in the apostolic breaking of the bread; its unity was
made perfect in the one and unique Lord's Supper. But the response of the Father to the invocation of the Spirit, this miracle
on God's part, awaits the preliminary miracle on man's part: the
point at which the *epiclesis* takes place requires the ultimate
ascesis of purity and transparence of human hearts. This is why
St. Peter exhorts: "How great should be your sanctity and your
prayer to hasten the day of the Lord." "He who knows in the

truth, loves in the fire," St. Catherine of Siena used to say, and the fire is the Holy Spirit. "A theologian is a man who knows how to pray," say the Fathers. Now, to pray with the Holy Spirit is to infuse the same words with an eschatological impulse: "to receive" in order to announce "the things that are to come", and so, from the scene of shipwreck to launch out into the deep sea of the Father's love for men.

"If two among you shall agree on anything that you ask. . . ." Two wills cannot come into perfect harmony except in a third term, in the will of the Father. It is in this agreement that Christ manifests his presence, and it is to this Christ-like harmony that the Father cannot refuse what is asked. Therefore, the question is not merely to agree on theological formulas alone, but to be at one inwardly with the will of the Father: then the aspiration toward doctrinal agreement will no longer be met with an impasse.

The ecumenical councils have conceived and forged dogmatic definitions as so many formulas that are primarily liturgical and doxological. This fact should make us attentive to their dimensions for prayer. The true spirit of criticism in a living theology, faithful to the innermost core of the thought of the Fathers, issues from the Holy Spirit with the purpose of "cleansing" or "purifying" and "demythologizing" *the* traditions and so to recover *Tradition,* that dazzling *Christophania* on which the Spirit descends in the form of a dove. Then it is possible to understand the primacy given to the evangelical *martyria,* and to the testimony of the martyr-Churches of our own day as they speak these words: "May the Holy Spirit guide us through the fiery furnace of these trials to the fuller manifestation of his glory." These thunderous words—but, even more, the silence in which they are shrouded—invite the Churches to self-purification by establishing themselves on the testing ground of crucified love. Side by side with the cerebrations of the theologians is to be found the magisterium of the martyrs and saints, with their theophanies of charity and light for the moment, which it would have been impossible to foresee.

V

For an Ecumenism of Epiclesis

Finally, it is the great concern of the East to have the West become aware of an *epiclesis* which is not simply one of the elements entering into the economy of salvation. *Epiclesis* springs from the correct theology of the Holy Spirit; stripped of an ill-understood "filioquism", it leads straight to the heart of the theology of the Fathers, to an Orthodox emphasis on the Trinity as the center of religious worship and experience. Thus, in the prayer for the candidates for the sacrament of confirmation, the bishop prays: "O God, seal them with the seal of this immaculate chrism [the seal of the gifts of the Holy Spirit]; they will bear Christ in their hearts and so become the dwelling place of the Trinity." This prayer shows the magnificent trinitarian balance which eliminates all monist emphasis: sealed by the Spirit, made Christ-bearers so as to be theophanic, they are temples "filled with the Trinity". According to the Fathers, Christ is the great precursor of the Paraclete; the Word takes flesh so that we may receive the Holy Spirit, St. Athanasius teaches. The Spirit manifests Christ, and both, in their two-faceted unity, reveal the Father and delineate the icon of the trinitarian mystery. For the East, this is always and everywhere the "guiding image".

Thus, St. John Damascene, in his *Confession of the Orthodox Faith,* lays down in clear and magisterial terms the patristic tradition: "The three divine persons have the same essential being; they are united not that they may be confounded with one another, but so as to contain one another mutually." Each divine person is a unique manner of containing the same essence, of receiving it from the others, of giving it to the others. Their absolute unity includes their absolute diversity.

In line with this "guiding image", with this majestic representation of the absolute divine Church or this "pre-eternal" trinitarian Council, each ecclesial assembly or Church is a unique manner of containing or holding the identical essence of truth, of receiving it from the others, or giving it to the others, and thus of

containing and retaining the other Churches in the circulation of
ecclesial charity. This "polyphonic" convergence, always modeled
on the heavenly image, excludes uniformity, absorption or subordination. The Father, according to the very firm teaching of
the Eastern Fathers, is the principle of trinitarian unity. The
Father ensures it without breaking the perfect equality of the
three persons, which excludes all subordinationist submission (a
heresy that was condemned), and his magnificent and royal position is: "He who presides in love."

In the great communion of perfectly equal Churches, as a
consequence of the fullness of the episcopal eucharist in which
each one is a Church of God, only one presides in love.

This is a particular charism to ensure the unity of all, a charism
of love after the manner of the Father, and for this reason with
justice stripped of all jurisdictional power over the others. If we
must speak of a "fundamental desire", perhaps the only one is
the patient expectation and the hope that one day the Church
of Rome will recover her ancient place and will be once again
surrounded and venerated by all the Churches, because she will
be the "one who presides in love".

This is the place to repeat the beautiful words of St. Gregory
of Nyssa, called by the second Council the "Father of Fathers":
"Divine power is able to find hope in the hopeless and a means in
the impossible." It is not the way which is impossible; the impossible is the way to the desired end, with the divine lover of
men who is the Father.

Arthur M. Allchin/*Oxford, England*

The Witness of the Anglican Communion

As is well known the Anglican Communion contains within itself a number of different tendencies or groups, and this means that it is never easy to write about the Anglican position in a fully representative way. Three tendencies within Anglicanism are clear from the time of the Reformation itself: (1) "Catholic" in the Anglican sense of that word, stressing the continuity of the Church's life and structure, and appealing to the whole of Christian tradition; (2) "Evangelical" or "Reformed", sharing the basic convictions and desires of the continental reformers; (3) for want of a better word, "Liberal", conscious of the heritage of Christian humanism, associated with such a name as that of Erasmus.

However, it is possible to exaggerate the extent of the divergences within our Communion. While it is true that some Anglicans would claim to be pure Calvinists and others would claim to follow the teaching of the Council of Trent, the great majority stand somewhere in between and seek in various ways to hold together elements of the Reformation with elements of the pre-Reformation teaching and tradition of the Church. However important the changes of the 16th century were, we do not think of our Church as dating from that time, and we are happy that the name of no one reformer has ever been attached to it. The present Archbishop of Canterbury reckons himself to be the hundredth holder of that See in succession from St. Augustine.

Anglicans are thus conscious of many of the tensions between Catholics and Protestants as existing within their own Communion, and they have never altogether lost the sense of belonging to a larger whole, the Catholic Church, of which their own provinces form only a small part. For these reasons they have always been concerned with the question of the restoration of visible unity, especially during the last century.[1]

What is the faith which can hold together so widely differing points of view? It is well expressed in some words of the Lambeth Conference of 1878. "United under one divine Head in the fellowship of the one Catholic and Apostolic Church, holding the one faith revealed in Holy Writ, defined in the Creeds and maintained by the primitive Church, receiving the same canonical Scriptures of the Old and New Testaments as containing all things necessary to salvation, these Churches teach the same Word of God, partake of the same divinely ordained sacraments through the ministry of the same apostolic orders, and worship one God and Father through the same Lord Jesus Christ, by the same holy and divine Spirit, who is given to those that believe to guide them into all truth." [2]

At best, the Anglican Communion has been conscious not so much of certain demands which it has to make over against other Churches, whether of East or West, as of certain truths and historical experiences to which it must bear witness. Some of these truths and experiences do not seem in the past to have been recognized by Rome, or at least not adequately. However, an Anglican would believe that they are necessary to the fullness of the faith and life of the Catholic Church, and he believes that he must hold them in trust for the whole Christian people.

Of these points we may briefly mention six.

---

[1] The question of unity has been to the fore in every Lambeth Conference since this meeting of the bishops of the Anglican Communion was inaugurated in 1867.

[2] R. Davidson (ed.), *The Six Lambeth Conferences 1867-1920* (London, 1920), p. 83.

1. *Authority in the Service of Freedom*

All authority in the Church has the character of service, since it derives from the authority of Christ. It is an authority that does not impose itself upon men, but frees them so that they may be their own true selves. The revelation of God does not destroy, but respects and fulfills the freedom of man. This conviction, which has been central in Anglican theological thinking at least since Richard Hooker (1554-1600), is amply illustrated in a recently published book by Bishop H. R. McAdoo.[3] In the 19th century it was the theme of much of the most representative Anglican theological writing, as for instance in F. J. A. Hort, *The Way, the Truth and the Life,* or in the symposium of essays edited by Charles Gore, *Lux Mundi.*

Throughout, Anglicans have sought to avoid too violent an opposition between God and man, and they have wished to understand further how God works *in* man. This is probably the reason for our constant attraction to the Johannine writings in the New Testament, and to the doctrine of the incarnation as defined at Chalcedon and expounded by the Greek Fathers. This too is the reason why we give what sometimes seems a scandalously large place to reason and historical inquiry in the Church's life, and why we emphasize so strongly the significance of given historical events and structures.

For this reason, too, we prefer to think of the authority of God as mediated within the Church through a variety of channels rather than as concentrated in one. ". . . described in Scripture . . . defined in Creeds . . . mediated in the ministry of the Word and sacraments . . . verified in the witness of saints and of the *consensus fidelium.* Liturgy, in the sense of the offering and ordering of the public worship of God, is the crucible in which these elements of authority are fused in the fellowship and power

---

[3] H. R. McAdoo, *The Spirit of Anglicanism: A Survey of Anglican Theological Method in the Seventeenth Century* (London, 1965). This book by the Bishop of Ossory is a very valuable contribution to the study of the subject.

of the Holy Spirit. It is the living and ascended Christ present in the worshiping congregation who is the meaning and unity of the whole Church. He presents it to the Father and sends it out on mission." [4]

Within the common life of faith and worship, the freedom of the scholar and thinker must be respected. Certainly the individual can misuse this freedom, but it is always dangerous to curb it by the use of externally applied authority. It is better if it can be restrained by a growing sense of the solidarity of the individual with the whole of the Church's life and worship, which is something prior to its dogmatic formulations. When the individual loses this sense of loyalty, of belonging to the Church's common life, then he himself cuts himself off from the household of faith. But since the members of the Church are primarily members of a family and not subjects of a judicial authority, a surprising variety and liberty should be allowed to them.

2. Complementary Approaches to Faith

Within the one household of faith it is possible for different schools of thought and spirituality to coexist and enrich one another. A thoughtful Anglican will not usually claim that the tensions and differences of view that exist within his Church are in themselves a model for other Christians to imitate. Rather, they are to be seen as a reflection of the unresolved problems of the whole of Western Christendom. However, he would maintain that they show at least something of the way in which different approaches to the mystery of faith and to the disciplines of Christian living can be complementary and not contradictory. A religion centered on the Bible and growing from intense personal devotion to the Savior need not necessarily be at war with a religion centered in the sacraments and rejoicing in the communion of saints. A biblical approach to theology which stresses the given quality of revelation can live together with a more philosophical approach that stresses the need to relate the revela-

[4] *The Lambeth Conference. 1948. The Encyclical Letter from the Bishops, Together with Resolutions and Reports* (London, 1948), p. 85.

tion given once for all to the whole of human experience and knowledge. In such a view of things the distinction between what is of faith and what is of theological opinion or popular devotion becomes particularly important, as it must also be in any perspective that looks toward the restoration of unity.

3. *The Bible Read through Tradition*

In making this distinction within tradition, between what is of faith and what, however important it may be, is secondary, the witness of the Bible is of decisive importance. Here the Anglican reformers are at one with their continental contemporaries. As Article VI of the thirty-nine Articles declares: "Holy Scripture containeth all things necessary to salvation: so that whatsoever is not read therein, nor may be proved thereby, is not to be required of any man, that it should be believed as an Article of the Faith, or be thought requisite or necessary to salvation." But this same Scripture is always to be read in and through tradition, and particularly in the light of the christological and trinitarian decisions of the first four General Councils.

Anglicans often speak of an appeal to the witness of the "primitive" Church (the first five centuries), or the "undivided" Church (the first ten centuries). Admittedly these terms are only approximate, but they point to an openness and balance in the understanding of the faith which was present in the earlier centuries of the Church's history but afterward obscured. This does not mean that the Church ceased to speak with authority after the schism of the 11th century, but it does mean that, in our thinking on this subject, we must take into account the life of the whole of historic Christendom since the schism and try to discern the common tradition existing despite the separation of the Churches.

This means, too, that we must pay special attention to the existence and witness of Eastern Orthodoxy. Have Western Christians in general, and Roman Catholics in particular, taken sufficiently seriously the claim of the Eastern Church to have maintained in principle this balance and this openness of the early centuries? Have we allowed the cultural remoteness and the empirical weakness of Eastern Christendom to blind us to the greatness of its claims on our attention? Shall we ever be able to understand the developments of the Western Middle Ages and to resolve the problems of the 16th-century divisions without a much deeper understanding of the causes of the earlier schism between East and West?

4. *Collegiality and Primacy*

This deep regard for the position of the Eastern Orthodox Churches is closely related to the Anglican attitude toward apostolic office in the Church. While it is evident that a Church which broke with the Roman See in the 16th century cannot regard the papal supremacy in the same way as Roman Catholics do, it is also evident that a Church which seeks "to continue" and "reverently use and esteem" the orders of bishops, priests and deacons, as inherited from the apostles' time,[5] cannot be indifferent to the concept of collegiality. Although the subject is one that has not been greatly developed by Anglican theologians, it is clear that in general they consider the college of bishops in the Church today as in some way corresponding to the college of the apostles in the beginning.

Authoritative writers can be found from the beginning of the 17th century onward who concede to the Bishop of Rome a primacy among the bishops that corresponds with the primacy of Peter among the apostles. What the exact nature and extent of that primacy is poses a difficult question from the Anglican point of view.[6] At the very least they feel that it should respect

[5] Cf. the Preface to the Ordinal in *The Book of Common Prayer.*

[6] Cf. the statement of the Anglican group at the Malines Conversations in May, 1925. "The Church is a living body under the authority of the bishops as successors of the apostles: and from the beginnings of Church history a primacy and leadership among all the bishops has been recognized as belonging to the Bishop of Rome. . . . The authority of the pope is not separate from that of the episcopate; nor in normal circumstances can the authority of the episcopate be exercised in disassociation from that of its chief. In virtue of that primacy, the pope can claim to

and maintain the legitimate diversity of the different local Churches, that it should confirm rather than eclipse the authority of the whole episcopal order, and that it should always be clearly distinguished from the absolute lordship of Christ within his Church.

5. Marian Dogmas?

The question of the authority of the Roman See naturally leads us to consider the very difficult question of the two Marian dogmas proclaimed since 1854. The Anglican Communion is perhaps the one place in Christendom where a considerable number of people who believe these doctrines live together in a single body with those who do not. Certainly, it is only a rather small minority who explicitly accept the two doctrines that have been defined, and even they would regard them not as primary parts of the faith, but as among "the highly probable secondary truths of our religion, having a due place in Christian devotion, in subordination to those truths that are primary".[7] But there would be many more who would be prepared to admit that Protestantism in general has lost greatly through the neglect of devotion to the Mother of God, and who would recognize that such devotion is a fitting and proper response to the unique role of Mary in the economy of salvation. They would desire to think of the Blessed Virgin always in relation to the incarnation of the Lord, our Lord and hers, and always as a type of the whole Church and of each believer.[8] In following such a line of approach, certain possibilities of a common and fruitful discussion open up in an area where final agreement still seems far distant.

---

occupy a position in regard to all other bishops that no other bishop claims to occupy in regard to him." G. Bell (ed.), *Documents on Christian Unity: Second Series* (London, 1930), pp. 36-7. Not all Anglicans would go so far as this.

[7] H. S. Box, "The Assumption," in *The Blessed Virgin Mary: Essays by Anglican Writers,* ed. E. L. Mascall and H. S. Box (London, 1963), p. 100.

[8] A. M. Allchin, "Our Lady in Seventeenth-Century Anglican Devotion and Theology," *ibid.,* pp. 73-4.

6. *Anglican Orders*

Finally, we must mention a matter that in the past has acquired a disproportionate importance in the relations between Anglicans and Roman Catholics: the question of Anglican orders. "Since", in the words of the Archbishops of England in 1897, "we firmly believe that we have been truly ordained by the chief shepherd to bear a part of his tremendous office in the Catholic Church",[9] it is natural that we should hope that this matter will eventually be reconsidered by the Holy See. The matter is not one that should be treated in isolation from the whole context of ecclesiology. Rather, it should be seen in the light of an altered evaluation of the fundamental intentions of the reformers, of a renewed and deeper consideration of the nature of priesthood in the Church, and of a further view of more recent developments in the Anglican Communion (including the participation of Old Catholic bishops in Anglican consecrations). The fact that a number of the Eastern Orthodox Churches have given a conditional recognition of the validity of these orders also seems significant.

It is clear that, in all the points that have been mentioned, the situation between Anglicans and Roman Catholics has been materially altered by the work of Vatican Council II. The reaffirmation of the centrality of Scripture in the tradition of the Church; the new emphasis on the Church as the People of God; the recognition of the possibility of many theological and liturgical traditions existing within the unity of faith; the renewed statement of the supreme importance of the liturgy for the Church's faith and life; the attempt to situate the papal supremacy within the context of the episcopal college and to see the hierarchy itself within the whole gathering of the Church; the new assessment of the ecclesial character of non-episcopal Churches; the fuller recognition of the importance of Eastern Orthodoxy; the decision to place the consideration of Marian

---

[9] *Responsio Archiepiscoporum Angliae ad litteras apostolicas Leonis Papae XIII. De ordinationibus Anglicanis* (with English translation) (London, 1897), p. 7.

doctrine within the *Constitution on the Church;* and last, but certainly not least, the new attitude toward the question of liberty in religious matters—all these developments are cause for deep thanksgiving from the Anglican point of view. They are moves in a positive direction.

If, in the past, the things for which we stood did not always appear to gain much recognition at Rome, the situation now is considerably altered. As for the future, much depends on the way in which the Council decrees are regarded. It is possible that if they were simply placed on one side as beautiful and impressive documents, nothing substantial would change in Anglican relations with Rome. However, if they are treated as a program for action and seen as stepping stones to further developments, then it is difficult not to think that they will lead in the course of time to a profound change in the situation between us, a change that will make it possible to envisage more clearly that restoration of unity which is so much desired.

Franklin Littell/*Chicago, Illinois*

The Concerns of the
Free 'Churches

I n a recent discussion of the popular Harris Survey, the editors
of *The Christian Century* have
attempted to interpret the significance of the prevailing popular-
ity of religion in the United States.[1] The facts are striking: "On
the basis of a projection of this poll, 97 percent of the population believes somehow in some sort of God; 83 percent claims
to contribute financially to a religious cause or to religious institutions; 72 percent believes in an afterlife; 75 percent claims
to go to church or synagogue at least once a month." The editors were primarily concerned with the theological problem.
This writer desires to accent the remarkably wide base of finan-
cial support and participation revealed.

The Harris Survey report coincides with the findings of other
studies. In the last century and a half, after the collapse of the
colonial State-Churches had left less than 10 percent of the
American population with any Church affiliation, Church membership has been brought to nearly 70 percent of the population.
Moreover, a governmental survey in March, 1957, showed that
96 percent of the American population fourteen years of age
and older claims religious affiliation.[2] Whatever the effect on

[1] "Poll Points to a Paradox," in *The Christian Century* 82 (1965), p.
1118.
[2] "Religion Reported by the Civilian Population of the United States:
March, 1957," in *Current Population Reports Series* 79 (Feb. 2, 1958),
p. 20.

quality of membership, the American pattern of religious liberty and voluntary religious association has proved to be—*quantitatively*—a huge success.

I

HISTORICAL DEVELOPMENT

For the first half of American history, the dominant Churches —Congregational in New England and Church of England in the middle and southern colonies—were imitative of the customs and relationships of the old world. State and Church cooperated intimately. Toward dissenters, governmental policy alternated between toleration and persecution. Maryland, under the Catholic Lord Baltimore, for a brief period practiced toleration, but later Puritan and Anglican regimes introduced repression again. Rhode Island, under Roger Williams and his successors, espoused separation of the political from the religious covenants, but "Little Rhody" remained a tiny nest of families out of sorts with New England's Standing Order, and had no real influence until the debates accompanying the ratification of the Federal Constitution (1789-1791). Only Pennsylvania, among the larger and influential settlements, under William Penn offered religious liberty and refuge to persecuted sectaries from the continent of Europe, but after Penn's death that government, too, introduced constitutional discrimination against Jews, Unitarians and Catholics. In short, American religious life—heavily dependent upon clergy trained in Europe—was part and parcel of European Christendom (British style).

With the founding of the republic, the base of operations shifted. The exemplary acts were the enactment of the Great Bill of Religious Freedom in Virginia (1784-1786) and the ratification of the First Amendment to the Federal Constitution. Rhode Island and North Carolina refused to ratify until religious liberty was recognized as a "natural right". The provision that "Congress shall make no law respecting the establishment of religion or prohibiting the free exercise thereof" was later incorporated in modified form into many state constitutions. In the modern period, religious liberty has by decisions of the United States Supreme Court come (through the "due process of law" clause of the Fourteenth Amendment) to control actions of lower governments (state, county and city) as well as federal.[3]

It took from 1774 (Virginia) to 1834 (Massachusetts) for religious liberty to be accomplished in law, and in many respects the older tradition of Protestant privilege has continued into recent times. Nevertheless, a standard was raised, and he who would understand the problems and possibilities of the "Free Churches" must consider carefully what was done in the shift from establishment to voluntarism at that time.

The transition was neither to toleration, which a number of colonial governments had attempted from time to time and found politically ineffectual and theologically presumptuous, nor to a *pax dissidentium*. The latter interpretation, popular with some secular historians, seeks to explain American religious liberty as a reluctant but necessary armistice between competing sects. This is not, however, what the decision-makers said of it. The debates in the Virginia House of Burgesses, and in the state conventions which ratified the Federal Constitution and the Bill of Rights, show quite clearly that they felt they were changing to a new and history-making relationship between Church and State. The change was not made by dogmatic anticlericals out of hostility to religion, but out of a conviction concerning the nature of high religion and limited government.

Patriots like George Washington and Patrick Henry opposed the separation of the political from the religious covenants because they did not believe that a stable society was possible without an established Church. Patriots like James Madison and Samuel Davies and James Monroe, however, had come to the conviction that only that service is pleasing to God which is

[3] Cf. F. H. Littell, *From State Church to Pluralism* (New York, 1962), and T. G. Sanders, *Protestant Concepts of Church and State* (New York, 1964), *passim*.

voluntary and uncoerced. They had come to feel that voluntary service and commitment were superior to any churchmanship enforced by law, and the revivals of religion which began with the Great Awakening (1734ff.) had convinced them that religious liberty was practical as well as principled.

To complete the historical picture, it should be noted that the experiment succeeded only because during the 19th century the leaders of the various religious bodies developed those "new methods" which won the people back to the Churches on a voluntary basis. In Protestantism, these methods were primarily directed to mass evangelism—from the "camp meetings" and Sunday School Movement to house-to-house visitation. In Catholicism, the parochial school system and the development of teaching and missionary orders reclaimed the people in exodus from State-Churches of America and Europe.

During the 19th century, and carrying on to the present, North America was missionary territory—just as truly as Africa, Asia and the islands of the sea. During this period the identity of American Christians—most of them "new Christians"—shifted from the complex of European Christendom to the style of the "Younger Churches" of the missions. Most of the problems that now confront the American Churches derive from the fact that most members are first-, second-, or at most third-generation converts. Racism, a vulgar materialism, an obsession with statistical success, a slovenliness of liturgy, a frequent uncertainty in creedal commitments—all are problems typical of a highly successful mission field. It is sometimes said that Europe is today in a "*post*-Christian era". America is, if anything, in a "*pre*-Christian era".

For some time the myth of "Christian America" was perpetuated, even though representatives of the missionary societies —both European and American—treated the territory for what it was: missionary area. The idea was strong that American Church life, both Protestant and Catholic, was still an extension of the old Christendom—long after the circumstances had so changed that the Church views of Luther or Calvin or Canisius were only by the most tortured reasoning relevant at all. Now, and largely as a result of recent scholarly work, documents are being published and monographs written that set the whole development in a different historical perspective altogether.[4] In sum, American Protestantism can no longer be conceived as a somewhat splintered or fragmented representation of the major lines of the "magisterial Reformation".[5] Its true archetype—as indeed discerned by a few scholars of the older generation, such as Kenneth Scott Latourette, Roland H. Bainton and William Warren Sweet—is to be found in the "Free Church" line of "the Left Wing of the Reformation" (Anabaptist and radical Puritan).

II

TESTIMONY OF CHRISTIAN LIBERTY

This fairly extensive summary of the historical development of the "Free Churches" in America may be useful for pointing up the importance of the Churches' present struggle to attain self-consciousness, a sure awareness of self-identity, as well as because these Churches are the largest blocs of world Christianity to have left the Constantinian era behind and undertaken the peril and promise of religious liberty. At the base of the experiment is a conviction about the nature of high religion. The other side of the coin is another conviction, almost as momentous, in the affairs of men: to abandon triumphalism and sacral politics in favor of secular and limited government.[6] Almost as compulsive as the view of the true Church among the forerunners of the "Free Church" was the view of good government.

[4] F. H. Littell, *The Origins of Sectarian Protestantism* (New York, 1964), Ch. V.

[5] Cf. G. H. Williams, *The Radical Reformation* (Philadelphia, 1962), pp. xxiii-xxxi.

[6] One of Reinhold Niebuhr's contributions was to establish and interpret the positive worth of "secular" government. A recent work that carries the argument significantly further is H. Cox, *The Secular City* (New York, 1965), Part I.

Good government is free of the ecclesiastical conspiracies and cabals of former times: without the need to cloak its actions in ultimates, it can simply govern. The true Church ("die rechte Kirche", in 16th-century terms) is free from governmental pressures and political manipulation which corrupted religion in former times: no authority shall be recognized except the Head of the Church (Jesus Christ); no power shall have sway except the Holy Spirit. There is a certain simplicity in such premises which leave unsolved all of the problems of the adjustment of political and religious powers and of the precise structures of the visible Church.

Nevertheless, it must be recognized that the section of Protestantism operating on such premises—premises that have to a certain extent been authenticated in the American experiment—is of a quite different kind from the Protestant establishments of Europe and their religious colonies overseas. Emphasizing the power of the Holy Spirit, these Churches have become a kind of "third force" in many mission fields—particularly in Central America and West Africa. Claiming to recapture the atmosphere and genius of the New Testament and Early Church (their slogan from the 16th century on being *restitutio,* not *reformatio*), these Churches enter the Catholic-Protestant dialogue at a quite different point from Anglicanism, Lutheranism or the Reformed Churches of the Continent. This most important point has indeed been noted and discussed in a very significant recent study by the American Catholic lay theologian, Michael Novak.[7]

III

CONTRIBUTIONS TO DIALOGUE

What then are the points at which the "Free Church" line of historical and theological development has something uniquely valuable to contribute in the emerging age of dialogue? Any one

[7] M. Novak, "The Free Churches and the Roman Church," in *Journal of Ecumenical Studies* II (1965), pp. 426-47.

of the questions now to be put on the record can be extensively documented and discussed, both in reference to concerns of Catholic colleagues in the dialogue and also in whole or partial distinction from positions advanced by representatives of "magisterial Protestantism". Although not always consistently or fully realized in practice, the following are basic teachings professed for four hundred years by men of the "Free Church" line in Protestantism. Since they professed to be in basic agreement with the chief theological emphases of the reformers (*e.g.*, "justification by faith"), no mention will be made of points where there is no substantial disagreement.

1. Church history is periodized on a primitivist[8] scale of golden age (Early Church), fall (Constantinian Era) and restitution (Free Church, sometimes limited in sectarian spirit to its own movement). The New Testament and Early Church mode and style of life are normative (suffering, non-resistance, eschatology).

2. The true Church is a visible company of brethren, bound together in a covenant of discipleship and for the perfecting of their witness.

3. Within the covenant-people, who have joined by believers' baptism or by adult repeating of vows made for them in infancy, Church discipline is maintained. Culture-religion, established by the promiscuous admission to membership of undecided and un-yoked individuals, is specifically condemned.

4. The faithful community shares a general ministry, mission and witness to which all the baptized are called. Those who hold functional offices are called by Christ to the building up of his Church, and they have no authority apart from the covenant-people.

5. The covenant-people practices "separation" from the spirit of the times, from the style of life of the dying age. This people strives to live a kingdom-of-God ethic, practicing mutual aid and condemning avarice and exploitation.

---

[8] Cf. "Primitivismus," in F. H. Littell and H. H. Walz (eds.) *Weltkirchenlexikon* (Stuttgart, 1960), cols. 1182-7.

6. From the human side, enrollment in the covenant is by voluntary decision; this is also the legal situation. Abstention is more worthy of an honest man than to mask inward unbelief by a show of outward conformity. Theologically speaking, the human act, which constitutes a congregation of faithful people, is in human response to the divine initiative.

7. Among the New Testament commands, none is more earnest than the Great Commission (Matthew 28, 18-20). (The Hutterite wing of the Anabaptists was the most energetic missionary section of 16th-century Protestantism. The expansion of the Protestant missionary effort has been largely based on the Free Churches.)

8. In the congregation and at higher levels of Church government, decisions are reached by the practice of open discussion in quest of consensus. Whoever may declare that a consensus has been reached, all of the believing people are involved in the process, and in the final sense it is the Holy Spirit who rules and on occasion overrules.

9. The Pauline missionary method of preaching and letter-writing is the only valid way of Christian persuasion: in matters of faith, governmental use of the sword or other forms of violence and coercion are specifically repudiated.

10. The separation of the religious from the political covenant frees the Church to be truly *Ecclesia viatorum,* and frees government to be a just government—secular, limited, modest in its claims (theologically speaking, a "creature").

Such are the historic Free Church concerns, many of them today the subject of discussion by brethren from other backgrounds and traditions.

Daniel O'Hanlon, S.J./*Los Gatos, California*

What Can Catholics Learn from the Free Churches?

Although there is no uniform definition of the Free Churches, and recent historical studies are revising our understanding of their origins, there is a cluster of concerns that are clearly enough identified as "Free Church". The common denominator that seems to link them all together is protest against an "establishment" that is condemned for having lost its spiritual vitality and degenerated into empty formalism. The groups most easily identified as Free Churches, then, are those linked in some way to the left wing of the Reformation, as it has often been called in recent years, or the radical Reformation, as Professor George H. Williams calls it.[1] These were the groups that reacted against an established Church aligned with the State.

On the Continent, the Anabaptists protested almost as vigorously against Protestant establishment, Lutheran or Reformed, as against Catholic establishment.[2] In England, even today, Presbyterians, who are not normally considered Free Churchmen in the United States, are considered as one of the four principal Free Churches (with Congregationalists, Baptists and Methodists) simply because they are not part of the Established

[1] George H. Williams, *The Radical Reformation* (Philadelphia: Westminster Press, 1962).

[2] Franklin H. Littell, *The Anabaptist View of the Church* (Boston: Starr King Press, [2]1958).

Church.[3] In countries like the United States the matter is more complex, since there exists no established Church to provide a foil for identifying the Free Churches. In this situation, those groups that protested against an establishment at a former time or in another part of the world, or both, are in some way in the Free Church tradition. However, as we saw in the case of Presbyterians, this norm is not entirely adequate, and it may be that in the present situation, if we use Troeltsch's socio-religious distinction between "Church" and "sect" as a guide, pentecostal-type Churches are the real Free Churches of our time.[4] The "establishment" against which they seem to be reacting draws its power and sanctions more from a continuing cultural community than from State support.

In any case, those elements in Protestantism that most set it apart from late medieval and Counter-Reformation Catholicism are found in more undiluted form in the Free Church tradition than in the classical Churches of the Reformation. That is why the term "radical Reformation" is so appropriate, and why the lessons that the Catholic Church can learn from Protestantism are put to us more clearly and dramatically by the Free Churches than by any other Protestant Churches.

The purpose of this article is not to criticize the deficiencies of the Free Churches, past or present. Such an approach does not imply a naïve blindness to their weaknesses; however, in ecumenical exchange we all profit most, and act most genuinely as Christians, if, as we meditate on the Gospel together, we try to learn from the others the lessons *we* need. This truth was well expressed in 1620 by the Free Churchman, John Robinson, in a sentence whose final clause has often been quoted, but whose neglected first half is no less important: "If God reveal anything to you by any other instrument of his, be as ready to receive it as if you were to receive any truth by my ministry, for I am

---

[3] Horton Davies, *The English Free Churches* (London: Oxford University Press, 1952), p. 41.

[4] D. J. O'Hanlon, "The Pentecostals and Pope John's New Pentecost," in *America* 108 (May 4, 1963), pp. 634-6.

verily persuaded that the Lord hath more truth yet to break forth out of his holy Word." [5]

As we try to learn these lessons, especially in the all-important exchange that must become normal at the parish level, we must cultivate an openness on both sides that will enable us not only to learn the more obvious lessons of which we will presently speak, but also to learn how to cope with the practical problems that arise when we try to apply these lessons in the concrete life of the Church. How, for instance, does one promote genuine responsibility and Christian freedom in each member of a local congregation without loss of community discipline? As the basic conciliar principle of shared Christian responsibility begins to find its way into the diocese and the parish with structures like diocesan and parish councils, the experience of the Free Churches can help us greatly if we will have the humility to draw upon it.

The lessons we can learn from the Free Churches can be outlined under five headings: (1) responsible living faith; (2) the local church; (3) the priesthood of all believers; (4) religious liberty; (5) openness to new forms.

1. *Responsible Living Faith*

Free Churchmen have always felt that institutional routine and formalism are the prime enemies of true Christianity. For this reason, Church membership, which follows from the mere fact of being born into a certain group, has been one of the principal targets of their criticism. The Baptist refusal to baptize infants, for instance, is one form of this protest. Because Baptists stress the need of an *adult commitment of faith*, they postpone baptism until a conscious free commitment of faith can be made by the prospective Church member. The concern that lies behind this practice is the same concern that has led an increasing number of Catholic pastors in some parts of the world to refuse baptism to infants brought to them by parents whose Christianity is purely nominal. Since the child has no prospect of being nur-

---

[5] Cited in Davies, *op. cit.,* p. 56.

tured in a Christian home where faith can blossom as the child matures, these pastors—wisely, it would seem—refuse to mock the sacrament of baptism by connivance with those for whom it is no more than a social celebration devoid of real religious meaning.

Perhaps a positive way for Catholic pastors to show the concern that lies behind the Baptist believer's baptism would be to develop the pastoral possibilities of the sacrament of confirmation in response to a suggestion of Schwenckenfeld made over four centuries ago: "If you won't agree to eliminate infant baptism, at least there should be set up a ceremony by which the baptized children, when they have reached the right age, will be dedicated to Christianity." [6] Confirmation has traditionally been associated with baptism, yet has been the object of greatly varied pastoral practice in both the age at which it is given and the aspect emphasized. Could it not be more explicitly made an occasion for the young adult freely, consciously and responsibly to ratify the faith whose seed was planted at baptism? St. Thomas held that every person born into this world—whether baptized or not—makes a fundamental option in his first serious moral choice.[7] Imaginative pastoral practice might make confirmation explicitly the occasion for a formal public act of Christian faith from the young baptized adult shortly after this becomes a real possibility.

Another aspect of the Free Church emphasis on responsible living faith can be seen in the Puritan emphasis on the covenant of "the gathered Church" and their refusal to submit to prescribed creedal statements. They remind us that the full reality of New Testament faith is much more than assent to a set of doctrinal propositions. St. Thomas is making a similar point when he writes that faith does not reach out merely to conceptual statements, but to reality, a reality that is nothing less than God

---

[6] Cited in Littell, op. cit., p. 36.

[7] Summa Theologiae I-II, q. 89, a. 6. For commentary on this text see Maurice Eminyan, S.J., The Theology of Salvation (Boston: St. Paul Editions, 1960), pp. 56-80.

himself.[8] The heat of Counter-Reformation controversy unfortunately led Catholics to put too exclusive an emphasis on faith as intellectual assent to conceptualized truths.

The Congregational emphasis on covenant can provide a healthy corrective for this unbalanced emphasis by reminding us that the deepest level of faith is that of the believer's total personal commitment to God in Christ. Indeed, no creed is properly understood unless it is the vehicle of the believer's covenant with God and with his fellow-Christians in the Church, for whom he assumes real responsibility. A proper understanding of this level of Christian faith also helps us to understand how we may find ourselves far more in unity with other Christians than we had dared to suspect, even across the boundaries of different formulations of the faith.[9]

It is not surprising that Free Church de-emphasis of set formulas is accompanied by a certain spontaneity and flexibility in worship and preaching the Gospel. Here the Catholic priest or bishop can find help in handling a new problem which has thrust itself upon him. Until recently, and especially in the Mass, he followed a pattern of worship that was fixed to the last detail. It is not surprising, then, that he often feels bewildered and ill-at-ease now that the renewed liturgy asks him to really "preside" at liturgical celebrations and gives him more and more personal responsibility in the choice of gestures and prayers in public worship to suit the time, the place and the congregation. The Free Church tradition can help him to find his way to a manner of leading the worshiping community which is personal, simple, meaningful and genuinely spiritual. The *Constitution on the Sacred Liturgy* has laid the theoretical foundations for all this, but Catholic pastors will see far more clearly what much of it

---

[8] *Summa Theologiae* II-II, q. 1, ad 2.

[9] "I should be inclined to say that the ineffable experience of the Word holds a certain precedence over its doctrinal statement." Avery Dulles, S.J., "The Theology of Revelation," in *Theological Studies* 25 (March, 1965) p. 54. "The saving movement of the soul, initiated by grace, can pass through formulas, themselves pitifully inadequate, or even glaringly false." Jean Mouroux, cited in Dulles, *loc. cit.*

means in actual practice through direct personal exchange with pastors in the Free Church tradition.

2. The Local Church

Free Churchmen, while not denying the reality of the universal Church, have always stressed the importance of membership in the *local congregation*. Late medieval and Counter-Reformation Catholicism, on the other hand, has emphasized membership in the universal Church. The danger to which Catholics are consequently exposed is a kind of abstract religion in which, through baptism, one becomes a member of the universal Church and is joined to all Christians across time and space, but in which, at the same time, responsibility to one's fellow Christians in the local congregation often seems unimportant. This Catholic deficiency becomes a matter of growing importance as Catholics all over the world are invited by Vatican Council II to renewal and reform within the Church and responsibility to other Christian Churches and the world.

The Free Church tradition invites us to remember that what is not local is not real. Although the bishops assembled in Rome can give—indeed have given—enthusiastic approval to a thoroughgoing program of Christian renewal, it still remains true that, until these things happen in local Catholic parishes, this renewal is nothing more than a paper theory. Free Churchmen remind us that the Church is not just an automatic ongoing *institution,* but an *event* that happens again and again in the worship and life of the local congregation. The presence of the Holy Spirit is not simply guaranteed by a legitimate succession of valid ministers and correct forms, but must always break through anew, especially as the assembly listens with faith to the Word of God and celebrates the eucharist. This can take place only in a particular local congregation.

Furthermore, responsible spokesmen for the Free Church tradition assure us that emphasis on the local congregation, far from promoting a spirit of individualism, stresses responsibility to others and community discipline.[10] The covenant is with the Lord and *with one another*. This horizontal communication and responsibility is expressed in worship. It also finds expression in the "church meeting" where mutual help and fraternal correction are exercised in the spirit of Matthew 18, 15-18.

This is not the place to enter into the complex problems that a depersonalized urban mass society poses for any pastor, Catholic or Protestant, who wants to build a genuine and responsible Christian community. However, concern for a vital local congregation and experience over the centuries in working to form it are part of the Free Church heritage on which we can draw.

3. *The Priesthood of All Believers*

When the Free Church tradition emphasizes the *priesthood of all believers,* this is not, we are told,[11] an attempt to demean the dignity of the ordained ministry by reducing all Christians to one low level. Rather, it is an effort to recognize the priestly dignity of all who through faith and baptism share in the priesthood of Christ. During the Counter-Reformation Catholics soft-pedaled the priesthood of all believers for fear of seeming to undercut the special role of the ordained priest. But the Council has now left those fears behind and returned to the sound Catholic tradition which makes the priesthood of all baptized Christians the basis of their full participation in the Church's worship[12] and

[10] "The Anabaptists . . . taught that in right living the Christians were *accountable for each other.*" Littell, *op. cit.,* p. 65. (Emphasis in original text.) "This means that one of the emphases of the Church covenant is upon the human mutuality. The exchange of promises is an exchange made by men with each other." John von Rohr, "In Historical Perspective: the Gathered Church," in *Perspectives on a College Church,* ed. Marilee K. Scaff (New York: Association Press, 1961), p. 78.

[11] "The priesthood of all believers was taken to mean the application of the *consilia perfectionis* to all Christians, instead of only a special class." Littell, *op. cit.,* p. 68. See Chapter V of the *Constitution on the Church,* "The Universal Call to Holiness in the Church" (Glen Rock, N.J.: Paulist Press, 1965).

[12] *Constitution on the Sacred Liturgy* (Glen Rock, N.J.: Paulist Press, 1964), n. 14.

their commission from the Lord himself to be his witnesses in the world.[13]

Here again, open exchange, especially at the local level, can help the Catholic pastor and his congregation to see the concrete implications of what the Council has already clearly affirmed. Catholic lay missionaries, who now realize that the "Great Commission" of Matthew 28, 19-20, is addressed to them, as well as to priests and religious, will learn much from the Free Churches who have always insisted on the missionary responsibility of *every* Christian.[14]

4. *Religious Liberty*

The first demand for full *religious liberty* ever written in the English language came early in the 17th century from the pen of John Smyth, the founder of the Baptists in England: "[We believe] that the magistrate is not by virtue of his office to meddle with religion or matters of conscience, to force or compel men to this or that form of religion or doctrine: but to leave the Christian religion free to every man's conscience, and to handle only civil transgressions, injuries and wrongs of man against man in murder, adultery, theft, etc., for Christ is the king and lawgiver of the Church and conscience." [15] The importance of this issue for the Catholic Church is so great that comment is hardly needed. As Professor Robert McAfee Brown has repeatedly said, there may be other issues that are of greater ecumenical importance in the long run, but there is no issue of greater *immediate* importance for the Catholic Church, nothing else so indispensable in creating an atmosphere of trust as she enters into exchange with the other Churches in search of Christian unity.

This issue of religious liberty is closely related to the current criticism by Catholic writers of the "Constantinian Church", the recognition that the Church lives in a state of diaspora, and the

[13] *Constitution on the Church* (Glen Rock, N.J.: Paulist Press, 1964), n. 33.
[14] Littell, *op. cit.,* pp. 109-37.
[15] Cited in Davies, *op. cit.,* p. 60.

emphasis placed on voluntary membership in a religious community. These have been familiar themes to Free Churchmen over the centuries. Here again, they can help us to learn how better to implement in practice what has already been accepted in theory. They can help us learn how to sustain the vitality of Christian communities in a pluralistic society without demanding or expecting the support of the State or even of the surrounding culture.

5. *Openness to New Forms*

When Pope John, at the opening of the Council, said that "the substance of the ancient doctrine of the deposit of faith is one thing, and the way in which it is presented is another", and when he went on to say that "it is the latter [the way in which it is presented] that must be taken into great consideration", he finally laid to rest the fear that had persisted among many Catholic theologians and churchmen since the Modernist crisis at the beginning of the century. They had been afraid that if they tampered with traditional formulas, the orthodoxy of their content would inevitably be endangered.

This *willingness to accept new forms* in doctrine, in worship and in evangelization has always been part of the Free Church tradition at its best. Yet, this openness has not sprung from a mere desire for novelty, but a yearning much like that expressed by Pope John in 1962 when he said that the work of the Council "is really directed entirely toward giving back to the face of the Church of Jesus the splendor and the pure and simple lines of its birth".[16] The simplified worship of the Puritans, the rejection of "canned prayers", the field-preaching of Wesley, the commissioning of lay preachers—these are all evidence of the Free Church desire to keep the spirit from being killed by the letter.

Now that Vatican Council II has initiated a program of renewal and reform, most of the basic concerns of the Free Church tradition have a foothold in the Catholic Church, at least on

---

[16] Cited by John O'Connor, in *The Monitor* (October 6, 1962), p. 4. See also Littell, *op. cit.*, pp. 79-108.

paper. These are all elements of the true Catholic tradition that have been neglected. If this movement of renewal and reform is to be made real in the Church (and history warns us that this is neither automatic nor guaranteed), the bare bones of the Council documents must take on flesh at the local level, in bishops' conferences, in dioceses and, above all, in local congregations. If bishops, parish priests and their congregations, theologians and seminarians will enter into an ongoing exchange with Christians of the Free Church tradition, sharing together in prayer and worship as far as possible, in dialogue, and in pastoral tasks for each other and for the world, they will find a continuing source of the stimulation they genuinely need.

Jorge Mejía/*Buenos Aires, Argentina*

Non-Catholic Missions in Catholic Countries?

The question in the title is perhaps of more direct pastoral relevance than any raised by the new situations obtaining in ecumenical theory and practice. Bishops and parish priests are generally ready enough to engage in ecumenical dialogue. Common tasks in the realm of the social order do not usually frighten them. Prayer and even liturgical services with other Christian bodies are sincerely accepted and promoted. However, the active presence of non-Catholic missionaries among their flocks appears to be going beyond the limit. How can we allow the faith of our own faithful to be disturbed, or, if it is dormant, to be awakened in a manner not strictly in accordance with orthodoxy?

The problem is a serious and a pressing one, and it must be delineated as clearly as possible, if we are to find some approach to a solution.

1. *A Duty of the Church, Not the State*

It must be stated at the outset that this problem is strictly one for the Church, and one which should be resolved through ecclesiastical channels. It would not be in accordance with present-day principles of religious liberty to have recourse to the State in order to prevent the entry of non-Catholic missionaries, at least those whose activities are evangelically correct. Such action hardly places the Catholic Church—which is a *universal* institution and cannot afford to forget the fact—in a favorable position to demand rights of entry to non-Catholic lands for her own missionaries. It may still be beneficial in some occasional particular set of circumstances, but in the long run it will entail three major disadvantages. The first is that such a solution, in the volatile social and political condition of the world today, is bound to be precarious. The second is that recourse to the "secular arm" can easily slip into neglect, or at least less assiduous cultivation, of the means of evangelization that belong properly to the Church. The third—and this is usually the basic disadvantage—is that it is usually inexact to call truly "Catholic" those who are Catholic in name only or by virtue of a partial practice of their faith.

2. *Mission and Proselytism*

True mission needs to be carefully distinguished from what is usually called "proselytism". A famous document produced by the World Council of Churches[1] establishes this distinction as clearly as possible. This article is concerned solely with the mission, which has its own religious and theological quality. The principles that govern it cannot be applied to the various forms of proselytism. This is a perversion, a *corruptio pessima* of something *optimum* for any Church: the proclamation of the name of the Lord. Bishops and parish priests have a perfect right to resist such abuses, although, if the proselytism they face uses calumny, they might be mindful of the words of the Lord himself: "Blessed are you when men revile you" (Matt. 5, 11).

It may be objected that it is not always easy to tell where missionary activity ends and proselytism begins. However, this objection strikes me as being based on an inaccurate analysis of the facts. One can in fact distinguish quickly and easily between proclamation of the Gospel by a non-Catholic Church and a mere hunt for converts, earthly and not heavenly in aim, negative in-

[1] Cf. *Evanston-New Delhi*, "Report of the Central Committee" (Neuchâtel, 1961), pp. 252-8 (*Témoignage chrétien: Prosélytisme et liberté religieuse*).

stead of positive, and bringing conflict instead of peace. Bishops and parish priests might be well advised to classify the religious communities and groups who are active in their areas into missionaries and proselytizers, and it will be the task of the ecumenical secretariats that will be set up in each region or nation to outline the principles governing this delicate question for the guidance of pastors.

3. *Non-Catholic Missionary Work: Good or Bad?*

So far I have only outlined what might be called the extrinsic limits of the problem. Theologically, this problem could be posed in the following terms: Are non-Catholic missions an *evil* or a *good*—in the sense of a partial good? There would seem to be two arguments, differing in nature and value, in favor of pronouncing them an evil. First, the preaching of non-Catholic Churches contains errors of faith; secondly, in Catholic countries or regions it tends to destroy Catholic unity. Therefore, it is an evil. But if it is an evil, it is one that can be tolerated, following the norms governing the moral attitude of tolerance (of which a papal exposition can easily be found, such as Pius XII's *Ci riesce*).[2]

However, it is possible to hold the other point of view, namely, that the preaching of non-Catholic Churches, at least in certain circumstances, is a good—a partial good, as are so many that form the course of our lives and govern our day-to-day conduct. The basis for this assertion is that authentic missionary preaching by non-Catholic Churches is, in its essential content, a preaching of Jesus Christ and an invitation to conversion to faith in him. It is also an announcement of the Word of God as contained in the Bible, with which the converted are placed in direct touch. Should the mission be an Orthodox one (rare in practice but worth considering as a hypothetical case), the positive content of its preaching will not be appreciably different from that of Catholic preaching and the sacraments administered will quite

[2] *A.A.S.* 45 (1953), pp. 788-9.

simply be ours. Therefore, under certain conditions, non-Catholic preaching and worship are not necessarily an evil.

What are these conditions? I should say that they can all be summed up in one basic condition. Those to be evangelized should lack easy and normal access to the sources of Catholic life. That is, they should be like "sheep who have no shepherd". In most cases they are in this situation through no fault of those who are at present responsible for them. It is just in countries once solidly Catholic, such as Latin America where evangelization was stopped by the stupidity of some men (by the suppression of the Jesuits, for example) and the ingenuous illuminism of others (such as when laicism was established in practically all parts), that the masses are today deprived of the Word and the sacraments, while the population continues to explode and the number of clergy decreases. This situation has been particularly typical of the great agrarian and pastoral expanses of Latin America, the plains and the foothills of the mountain ranges, but today the same conditions are extending to the industrial zones of the cities, the squalid shantytowns and the mining areas. As a general rule the inhabitants are all still baptized into the Catholic faith, but this is the beginning and the end of their vital participation in the Church. We know that this incomplete christianization, foreseen to be incomplete and beyond our resources to complete, poses numerous and grave problems. And now, supposing that non-Catholic missionaries, with sufficient credentials and intentions to carry out an authentic, even though limited, evangelization, appear in the midst of those "half-faithful", what are we to say? Shall we say that a total lack of religion, or superstition, is preferable to a certain measure of conversion to Christianity? From this basic principle we must conclude that non-Catholic missions are either an evil that can become tolerable, or a good that in certain circumstances should be welcomed.

The *Decree on Ecumenism* recently promulgated by Vatican Council II does not deal with this question specifically, but it does contain a statement that helps to elucidate it: "It follows that the separated Churches and Communities . . . have been by no means deprived of significance and importance in the mystery of salvation. For the Spirit of Christ has not refrained from using them as means of salvation. . . ." [3] If non-Catholic Churches and Communities have a meaning in the divine plan and can be used as a means of grace, it is difficult to deny to them on principle all access to the exercise of a legitimate missionary function.

This last affirmation raises the difficult theological problem of the legitimacy of non-Catholic missions, but this is not the place to go into it. We can for our present purpose content ourselves with stating a principle whose strict analysis could lead to a solution. The Catholic Church recognizes that the existence of other Churches and Communities has a valid place in the divine plan. In that case, can a Church have a valid existence as a Church without announcing the kingdom of God: in other words, without a certain amount of missionary activity? The form of the question has been basically modified by the new ecumenical, doctrinal and practical situation of today, and it is this situation that we must now examine.

4. Where Do We Go from Here in Practice?

The ecumenical situation means, at the very least, that the different Churches and Communities now recognize each other as such. This recognition provides important pointers to the practical solution of the problem.

In the wider field of missions to non-Christians, it is possible to envisage a sort of agreement by which each Church or Community could recognize certain fields of action as belonging to a particular unit, and would agree not to interfere in this field unless the Church responsible for it proved incapable of carrying out her mission there, either through incompetence or sheer lack of resources. The Catholic Church would not abandon her right and duty to proclaim what she holds to be the one true Gospel throughout the world, but she would recognize the existence

[3] Cf. *Decree on Ecumenism*, Art. 3 (Glen Rock, N.J.: Paulist Press, 1965), p. 51.

and the similar right of the other Churches, while taking into account their particular concrete limitations.

In the deliberately restricted context of traditionally Catholic countries or regions considered here, the new situation seems to require particularly close attention from the responsible bodies involved. The Protestant or Orthodox preacher will, in fact, be addressing congregations of faithful baptized into the Roman Catholic faith. Their religious background, however slight, will therefore be Catholic and, theoretically at least, they can be expected to grow to maturity in the Catholic faith. Can this fact be overlooked from the ecumenical point of view? It seems to me that the Church concerned must take serious account of it.

The difficult point is how. It neither will nor can make these people Catholic. But could it not perhaps prepare the way for Catholic evangelization by preaching common Christian truths and showing respect for local traditions in such fields as sacramental and mariological practices? The possibility of individual or even collective conversions cannot be discounted, but the main issue is whether such evangelization would be aiming to "convert" some of the people from one Church to another, or to convert all who have been baptized to the reality of their baptism and, through this, to fidelity to the Lord of all. In the ecumenical climate now coming into being, this is surely not too improbable.

Approaching the same situation from a different angle, there is another important consideration. The missionary in traditionally Catholic countries is not preaching in a sociological vacuum. However tenuous the knowledge of the faith and Christian practices may have become, the individual's subconscious and collective modes of behavior will be permeated by Catholicism.[4] However distorted the residues of a life of faith, they will contain potentially fertile elements and form a sort of fine web of personal and collective support. Should the individual really be presented with a chance to choose to break with all this? Faith,

[4] I am thinking of the situation obtaining in rural areas in particular, where primitive conditions have been more completely maintained. In the towns the general temper is one of radical paganism which extends also to men and women baptized in the Catholic faith.

as we know, transcends all human institutions and can never be reduced to their level; nevertheless, it creates institutions and does not exist without them. If they are disregarded, surely there is a risk of alienating the people thus torn out of their institutional context. Faith itself must of course always have the right to pass judgment on these institutions, but its judgment can be made in the light of respect for what is authentically and typically Catholic.

In practice, then, the Churches must together find some way of approach to this problem of missions in countries formerly united in the faith. This will need resources of both loyalty and charity and require the establishment of permanent consultative bodies in which questions, both of principle and of practical application, can be discussed. In this, as in so many other matters, frank and far-seeing conversations are the way toward really constructive solutions. Happily, all the Churches concerned are beginning to be favorably disposed toward such conversations. The most important single element in their disposition as it affects this problem is mutual recognition. Only if the different Churches and Christian Communities recognize each other as such is there hope that they will come to see each other as "means of salvation",[5] and to impose some voluntary limitation on their own activities for the sake of the greater good of the kingdom to which they all witness in such different ways. With this new spirit, faithfully inspired by the Spirit, the mission fields, which were usually a source of disharmony, could become a new and important link in the chain stretching toward unity.

[5] Cf. *Decree on Ecumenism,* p. 51.

PART II

BIBLIOGRAPHICAL
SURVEY

Maurice Villain, S.M./*Paris, France*

The Debate on the Decree on Ecumenism

The fact that I have arranged this survey around the conciliar *Decree on Ecumenism* does not mean that I intend to make the Roman Catholic position the pivot on which all the present events are turning—that would be a great mistake. I have simply taken this great text as the central reference because in the present context it is the principal document, and as such has acted like a magnet for almost all the ecumenical literature that appeared in 1965.

I

SHORT HISTORY OF THE DECREE

1. *The First Text (1963)*[1]

I must briefly recall the origin of the Decree (called in Latin: *Unitatis redintegratio,* the restoration of unity). It is a second draft. A first schema had been proposed on November 18, 1963, which was itself a combination of three documents, based on a

---

[1] The best general study on the Decree at present is that by Cardinal Jaeger, *Das Konzilsdekret über den Ökumenismus: sein Werden, sein Inhalt und seine Bedeutung* (Text in Latin and German, with commentary, Paderborn, 1965, 173 pages). It is very informative on the transition from the first text to the second, the debates and the voting.

text prepared by the Secretariat for Promoting Christian Unity (the original text of this document has remained unknown); then there was a text, *De Ecclesiae Unitate,* drafted by the preparatory commission for the Eastern Church and printed in the first series of the *Schemata Constitutionum et Decretorum* (this was mainly concerned with the Orthodox Churches); and, lastly, there was a chapter, *De Oecumenismo,* to be incorporated in the first schema on the Church. Although the two last texts were rather inadequate, Cardinal Bea had been asked to use certain parts of them in his new draft which, one presumes, had been rather spoiled by them.

As it then stood, the schema[2] consisted of five chapters. Three of these referred to ecumenism strictly so-called, under the titles: (1) principles of Catholic ecumenism; (2) practice of ecumenism; (3) Christians separated from the Catholic Church. The fourth dealt with the relations of Catholics with non-Christians, especially the Jews, while the fifth dealt with religious liberty. These last two chapters were to be detached later on.

This first draft proved frankly inadequate: it was not definite in style and it was not ecumenical. It started from the Roman Church as the center of such activity, and it was addressed to the separated Christians as individuals instead of as communities. Nothing was said about the method and norms for a dialogue or about the contents of prayer for unity. To the surprise of the Secretariat and the observers, the debate was sharp, constructive and fruitful. Of the amendments proposed [3] only those were retained that aimed at definite progress in the text; none that looked backward were retained. And so, the second draft of the Decree, considerably improved, was not subjected to any changes during the third session before its solemn promulgation on November 21, 1964.

---

[2] *Schema Decreti de Oecumenismo,* in three installments (April 22, 1963), and the *Relatio super schema Decreti de Oecumenismo* by Cardinal Cicognani, Bishop Martin, Bishop Bukatko, Cardinal Bea and Bishop De Smedt.

[3] Of the 1,300 *modi* proposed, only 28 were accepted, all of which improve the text.

2. The Second Text (1964)[4]

I am not attempting here a systematic analysis of this great text of which so many excellent commentaries already exist; I limit myself to its spirit and its most salient points. In this I shall make use of the best studies of specialists together with my own impressions, but their very agreement makes it unnecessary to distinguish between them.[5]

[4] *Schema Decreti de Oecumenismo* (April 27, 1964) and the *Relatio super schema emendatum Decreti de Oecumenismo* (by Bishops Martin, Helmsing, Hermaniuk and Cardinal Heenan). The typography of this second draft was inferior to that of the others: the first text was not printed facing the second so that it was difficult to trace the modifications. The definitive text, hastily printed during the night of November 19-20, with the 19 *modi* inserted by order at the last moment, does not carry the words *"de quo agatur in sessione publica die 21a novembris"* (for promulgation at the public session of Nov. 21) because the promulgation was still in doubt. There is a translation produced by the Catholic Truth Society, but a more accurate one with commentary by Fr. Bernard Leeming is in course of publication.

[5] The following list does not pretend to be exhaustive: A. Bea, "Il Decreto conciliare sull'Ecumenismo: contenuto et significato," in *Civiltà cattolica* (Dec. 19, 1964), pp. 524-34; "Il decreto conciliare sull'Ecumenismo: l'azione da svolgere," in *Civiltà cattolica* (Jan. 2, 1965), pp. 9-22; "Contributo del Concilio alla causa dell'unione dei cristiani," in *Civiltà cattolica* (March 6, 1965), pp. 422-34; "Prospettive del Segretariato per l'Unione dei cristiani," in *Civiltà cattolica* (June 5, 1965). The same optimism shows in an anonymous article, "Immobilismo cattolico nel dialogo ecumenico," in *Civiltà cattolica* (Jan. 16, 1965), pp. 105-8; W. Becker, "Das Konzilsdekret 'De Oecumenismo,'" in *Una Sancta* (2/3, 1965), pp. 83-100; G. Caprile, S.J., "Aspetti positivi della terza sessione del Concilio," in *Civiltà cattolica* (Feb. 20, 1965), pp. 317-41. First-hand information on the crisis of the last days and the attitude of Paul VI in his effort to accommodate the minority at the Council in order to maintain total impartiality: Y. Congar, "Bloc-notes," in *Informations catholiques internationales* (Sept. 15 till Dec. 1, incl.). These articles have been published in one volume, *Le Concile au jour le jour* (Paris, 180 pp.). Congar has also given an excellent introduction to the Decree (Ed. du Centurion, pp. 165-92); C. J. Dumont, "Le décret conciliaire sur l'oecuménisme: quelques réflexions en guise d'introduction," in *Vers l'Unité chrétienne* (Dec., 1964), pp. 93-5; Cardinal Jaeger, *op. cit.;* O. Rousseau, "Sur la IIIe session du Concile," in *Irénikon* 4 (1964), pp. 508-23; T. F. Stransky, *The Decree on Ecumenism of the Second Vatican Council.* Transl. and comm. (Glen Rock, N.J.: Paulist Press, 1965), 86 pages; G. Thils, "Le décret conciliaire sur l'oecuménisme," in *Nouvelle Revue théologique* (March, 1965), pp. 225-45; M. Villain, "La troisième session de Vatican II et le dialogue oecuménique," in *Rythmes*

(a) *Introduction*. All commentators have recognized the great grace which the ecumenical movement represents for our time, the discreet homage paid to the World Council of Churches (indicated by the terms of its doctrinal basis: the invocation of the triune God and the confession of Jesus as Lord and Savior), and the whole treatment of the text on the level of "communion" (everything is formulated on the level of "Churches", "communions" and "ecclesial communities", and no longer on that of individual Christians as in the first draft).

(b) *Catholic Principles of Ecumenism* (Ch. I). Many have noticed the right note struck by this title. There is only one ecumenism or ecumenical movement in which the Roman Catholic Church has her place with her own principles, just as the other Churches or communities take part in it on the basis of theirs. These principles of the Catholic faith are expressed here in exclusively biblical terms and follow the *Constitution on the Church*. The conclusion states in regard to the projection on this earth of the mystery of the Trinity: "Such is the sacred mystery of the Church's unity." The relations between our separated brethren and ourselves are no longer conceived in legalistic terms, but rather in those of theological values. After stating that baptism incorporates all Christians in Christ (understood as the "body of Christ") and therefore maintains a "certain communion", the text adds that many constitutive and vivifying elements of the Church "are capable of an existence beyond the confines of the visible Catholic Church". It is recognized that many "sacred actions" performed among our separated brethren are genuine means of grace and salvation, and that their communities are included in the mystery of salvation while the Spirit of Christ uses them as such. And if the Catholic Church remains

---

du Monde 4 (1964), pp. 273-92, esp. pp. 282-7; J. Willebrands, "Le mouvement oecuménique à l'heure du Concile," in *Vers l'Unité chrétienne* (March-April, 1965). See also the study of the Decree published by K. McNamara, E. McDonagh and J. Good (Catholics) in *The Irish Theological Quarterly* (April, 1965), pp. 129-56, with the rather personal reaction of F. E. Volkes (Anglican) on p. 156.

conscious of possessing—by right—the fullness of the gifts of Christ, she admits that she is far from reflecting this plenitude in the eyes of the world, and that the mystery of unity is not therefore limited to what this Church is in actual reality. This Church herself needs to enter into a fuller communion of the mystery of Christ. By the same token, the road of "return" or "integration" has shifted to a way of "communion". By these simple words one can judge how profoundly has been affected the classic Catholic mentality which was so alien, not to say hostile, to this kind of language.

(c) *Ecumenism in Practice* (Ch. II). This chapter is considered the main achievement of the Decree. French commentators, as well as Cardinal Jaeger, have detected here the influence of Abbé Couturier, the pioneer of spiritual ecumenism, and also the new light thrown upon all this matter by experience.

All are involved in this ecumenism, faithful and pastors; this remark at the outset proves sufficiently that ecumenism is not a matter for specialists, but is rather an aspect of the life of the whole Church. The pilgrim Church must constantly renew herself, be in a state of constant reformation, and all the present renewals contribute to this progress. There is no ecumenism without conversion of the heart and holiness of life. We must ask God and our brethren for forgiveness for all the faults committed against unity, and we must live according to the Gospel. Our prayer must be "unanimous" and must be, above all, "that prayer for the unity of the Church which the Savior himself addressed to the Father on the eve of his death, 'that all may be one' " (John 17, 21). It is easy to construct a whole theology of prayer for unity, such as Abbé Couturier advocated, "for the unity which Christ wants, with the means Christ wants" and for "the *sanctification* of all groups of Christians", since they are all committed to "spiritual emulation". It is comforting to notice that the delicate question of *communicatio in sacris* (sharing in the sacred rites), until now wholly rejected by the theology and discipline of the Church of Rome, is now an "open" question in a legislation which must still be defined and which is left to the judgment of the local bishop (the decision is left exclusively to the national conferences of bishops and, of course, the Holy See).

The text recommends the serious study of the mentality of our Christian brethren (their teaching, history, spiritual life, worship, religious psychology, culture, etc.), which, as our commentators observe, implies new associations and, on the intellectual level, the foundation of chairs of ecumenism in our theological faculties, with the possibility of offering these chairs to Protestant, Anglican or Orthodox professors, and the starting of interdenominational meetings of a doctrinal character on equal footing (*par cum pari*). Due allowance being made, the same reforms and principles hold for teaching in the seminaries and in missionary countries. Finally, the wish is expressed that there should be general cooperation among the Christian Churches on the social level, particularly in helping the underdeveloped countries, with the recommendation that, as far as possible, they demonstrate to the world their belief in the mysteries they hold in common, so that "the face of Christ the servant" may stand revealed to the world.

(d) *Churches and Ecclesial Communities Separated from the Roman Apostolic See* (Ch. III). All the commentators underline in this third and last chapter the praiseworthy effort made by those who drafted it to look at the Churches and ecclesial communities separated from the See of Rome objectively and from within, and no longer by comparing them with the fullness of the Catholic Church, which was the great defect of the first draft. The paragraph on the Eastern Churches is handled with particular care, and there is a new reference to the *communicatio in sacris* (here in the sense of a true *intercommunion*): "in certain favorable circumstances" and "with the approval of the ecclesiastical authority" this is not only considered "possible", but "desirable". As to the matter of dialogue, this is recommended on a basis of wide variety and therefore of pluralism: liturgical, disciplinary, theological dialogue. This noble text was obviously influenced by the meeting between Paul VI and Athenagoras I in Jerusalem.

The paragraphs dealing with the communities of a Protestant character cover only two and one-half pages in the original. They have not been treated in detail because of their extreme diversity, and only their main common elements have been underlined, but these few remarks are fair and carefully directed toward a much wished-for dialogue. The points mentioned are the profession of a christological faith in these communities and their love (and study) of the Scriptures. Taking due account of their various interpretations of the relationship between Scripture and the Church, the Bible should be the basis of the dialogue between them and us. Baptism, the Lord's Supper, Christian life, moral and social questions, etc., should constitute the principal matter for this dialogue, and all this together is a great step forward.

The Decree is but a starting point. This is the opinion of the commentators. And I quote the remarkable paragraph at the end which sanctions from now on the dynamic movement of an institution destined to surpass its own limits, urged on by the Spirit: "This sacred Council firmly hopes that the initiatives of the sons of the Catholic Church joined with those of the separated brethren will go forward, without obstructing the ways of divine providence, and without prejudging the future inspirations of the Holy Spirit. Further, this Council declares that it realizes that this holy objective—the reconciliation of all Christians in the unity of the one and only Church of Christ—transcends human powers and gifts. It therefore places its hope entirely in the prayer of Christ for the Church, in the love of the Father for us, and in the power of the Holy Spirit. 'And hope does not disappoint, because God's love has been poured forth in our hearts through the Holy Spirit who has been given to us'" (Rom. 5, 5).

As Yves Congar has said, the *Decree on Ecumenism* is more than a text, a teaching, a rule of behavior or action; it is a "deed", and this deed "has bearings comparable to the great historical decisions that have decided the course of events for centuries afterward".[6]

_____
[6] Preface to the Decree (Ed. du Centurion), pp. 189-90.

II

REACTIONS OF THE SEPARATED BRETHREN

The reactions of our separated brethren to the Decree are in every way comparable, both in number and in quality, with those of Catholic theologians.[7] Praise has been generous and has occasionally been expressed in striking terms; however, there have also been criticisms, and it is these, above all, that are useful to us, like the questions that have been asked. It is most important that we read the Decree in full awareness of these brethren, since there particularly we touch "the other's part" in the ecumenical problem and we can see better how the weaknesses of our text can be overcome some day. I have brought together a few of these reactions from among those that were rather typical. After a few comments of a general nature, I shall list first what is positively approved, and then the reservations and demands for further explanation.

1. General Comments

The general comments on the importance, novelty and boldness of the Decree show an impressive agreement. I am concentrating on the Protestant and Anglican reactions, but it will be useful to also add some Orthodox comments.

H. ROUX (of the Reformed Church): "Bold and new . . . a

---

[7] I mention as particularly instructive the various *Comments on the Decree on Ecumenism* by H. Roux (Ref.), pp. 104-7; O. Cullmann (Luth.), pp. 93-5; J. R. Chandran (Ch. of S. Ind.), pp. 101-4; R. McAfee Brown (Un. Presb. U.S.A.), pp. 95-7; J. Miguez Bonino (Meth.), pp. 109-12; O. Tomkins (Angl.), pp. 107-9; P. Evdokimov (Orth.), pp. 97-101: in *The Ecumenical Review* (April, 1965). To this should be added H. Roux, "Le décret sur l'Oecuménisme," in *Etudes théologiques et religieuses* 1 (1965), pp. 7-14; "Pour un dialogue exigeant," in *Réforme* (Oct. 24, 1964); *Le Concile et le dialogue oecuménique* (Paris: Ed. du Seuil, 1964); J. Bosc, "La Constitution sur l'Oecuménisme; réaction protestante," in *Amitié* (June, 1965), pp. 4-6; J. M. Hornus, "L'oecuménisme catholique et la troisième session de Vatican II," in *Christianisme* (Jan.-Feb., 1965), pp. 73-84; O. Cullmann, "Les portes ouvertes," in *Réforme* (Oct. 31, 1964); G. Richard-Molard, "Le drame catholique, Vatican II, positions protestantes," in *Réforme* (Oct. 17, 1964); "Espérance malgré tout," *ibid.* (Nov. 14, 1964); *L'hiver de Vatican II* (Paris, Albin Michel, 1965).

turning-point . . . a surprising and unexpected change." In order to appreciate the Decree at its true value, it should be read and interpreted "in the light of a twofold historical context: *that of the period preceding the Council* compared with which it definitely marks a point of arrival, a stage, an achievement; and *that of the conciliar period and the immediate future* for the *post-conciliar* ecumenical dialogue, compared with which it is a starting point, a new sense of direction for the theology and ecumenical activity of Catholicism".

As such it constitutes for the other Churches "a stimulating appeal, a challenge to critical and constructive reflection".

The Decree must be understood "in the light of its origin and of the difficulties which the Secretariat for Promoting Christian Unity had to overcome from the beginning until the end, up to the eve of the final vote, ever since it had been put in charge of it in 1962".

O. CULLMANN (Lutheran): "What has to be stressed with regard to all the schemata of the present Council holds particularly for the *Decree on Ecumenism,* namely, that the will to achieve a renewal, which inspires it from the beginning until the end, is still more important than the actual text. On this point I wholly agree with Fr. Congar's words that it is not just a text; it is a deed."

J. R. CHANDRAN (Church of South India): "This is a considerable step forward in the relations between the Roman Church and the other Churches, for which we have to be grateful to God. This document should be carefully studied by all the Churches. . . ."

R. MCAFEE BROWN (United Presbyterian Church of the United States): This observer sees in the Decree only an "interim document" reflecting the present thought of the Catholic Church, and he is astonished by this remarkable result which goes far beyond the dreams of the most advanced "romantic ecumenists" of two or three years ago.

J. MIGUEZ BONINO (Methodist): "One may say that [the Decree] embodies the spirit of the Council", which is "a spirit of

brotherly open-mindedness toward other believers", "of a burning desire for Christian unity and of a firm determination to promote it. In this sense the Decree is the natural outcome of the
Council".

O. TOMKINS (Anglican Bishop of Bristol): This author takes
the *Constitution on the Church,* together with the ecumenical
Decree which belongs to its scope, and is full of praise. Of the
principles formulated in Chapter I, he writes: "Everything is seen
in the light of the Scriptures, and I subscribe to everything except
the supremacy of Peter." Beyond this there is not one criticism or
reservation.

P. EVDOKIMOV (Orthodox): "The Decree . . . is more than
a 'reform'; some of its expressions are 'revolutionary' compared
with a still recent past. . . . In the present situation the Roman
Church has taken a step which touches the limit of her present
possibilities, considering the extreme tensions of her internal
tendencies. One should sincerely rejoice in this and give full credit
to the frequently heroic effort made by the fathers of the Council.
The text is an opening, an invitation to a dialogue, an appeal to
all to take an active part in it, so that we may all together break
the many kinds of deadlocks that have accumulated in history."

2. *Positive Aspects of the Decree*

(a) *The Extension of the Ecumenical Movement.* The Roman
Church "recognizes the ecumenical movement *de facto* as a sign
of the times", "as a spiritual event, the manifestations of which
are not exclusive to the Roman Catholic Church and go beyond
her institutional framework"; it is "a divine appeal of grace to
which Catholics should be capable of responding" (H. Roux, J.
Bosc).

(b) *The "Communal" Aspect.* The Roman Church now takes
seriously "the Churches and ecclesial communities" separated
from herself; she recognizes them as "means of salvation" which
make their members "partakers of a certain communion in
Christ". This goes well beyond the classic idea of a "return to the
fold" (H. Roux).

This feature has struck all the observers. O. Cullmann writes: "The goal of ecumenism is no longer our 'return' "; without any mental reservation, the charismata of non-Catholics are recognized as such, and the text reminds Catholics that these charismata can help toward a constantly more perfect penetration into the mystery of Christ and the Church." This opens up many consequences. Cullmann continues: "Henceforth one can meet certain practices, up till very recent times common in countries where the Catholics are a majority, with an official text that explicitly condemns them." On this point, Pastor G. Richard-Molard relates, not without humor, an incident that occurred during his stay in Rome for the third session. While he was walking with some experts, the latter boasted of the progress made in the ecumenical attitude even among our people. The conversation was about how to check certain devotional practices. He deliberately led their steps to the church of the Minerva where they saw women, children and old people indulging in their exuberant devotions at the foot of a statue of the Madonna. In their confusion the experts wondered how to put across the texts of the Council to the *popolino,* the little people, and how many generations would pass before such a check would be effective.

(c) *Charity, Repentance and Mutual Forgiveness.* Where division is mentioned, "there is not a single reproach", "not a single condemnation", and all "are brothers in Christ", H. Roux notes with pleasure, and J. Bosc with him. Cullmann and Chandran point to "various paragraphs that are obviously inspired by the inaugural address of Paul VI at the opening of the second session on the need for repentance and mutual forgiveness".

And Chandran adds: "A difficult question in the discussions, even within the World Council of Churches, is that of sin in the Church. The document shows a remarkable change in attitude. It is admitted that during her pilgrimage on earth 'the Church remains liable to sin in her members' (Art. 3). It is also emphasized that the Johannine statement about the universality of sin (1 John 1, 10) refers also to sins against unity, and the need of Catholics to pray to God for forgiveness of their sins of disunity is openly admitted" (Arts. 3 and 7). It is somewhat difficult to see that ideas, which had for a long time been accepted by professional ecumenists, were seized upon with such astonishment by outside observers; the reason is that they saw them for the first time mentioned in an *official* document of the Roman Church.

(d) *The Theology of "Values"*. All praise the new approach to problems that underlies the Decree, that theology of "values" which is gradually replacing scholastic and juridical theology. J. Miguez observes: "The *Constitution on the Sacred Liturgy* introduced a wedge into a juridical ecclesiology to make it yield; the same happened in the chapter on the People of God in the *Constitution on the Church* and the rejection of the two sources of revelation. The *Decree on Ecumenism* ratifies this more open kind of ecclesiology." H. Roux notes: "The analysis of the causes of separation and the listing of positive Christian values, preserved or developed in the large communities separated from full communion with the Catholic Church, shows the care taken to do away with every trace of polemics and the spirit of the Counter-Reformation." Oliver Tomkins is impressed by the new vision of Church membership and the recognition of ecclesial and institutional values in the various denominations. R. McAfee Brown comments on the words of the text where the Holy Spirit is said to use these communities and their "sacred actions", and that he is recognized to be active in the celebration of their eucharist. However, he wishes that this part played by the Spirit were more clearly defined by Rome. Nevertheless, it is good to know that the Spirit acts *through* these communities, and not *in spite of* them.

(e) *The Rejection of a False Irenicism*. The fact that the Catholic Church clearly proclaims her consciousness of being the Church of Christ does not upset Roux, Cullmann or McAfee Brown. On the contrary, they see in it a guarantee for the dialogue. Cullmann insists on it without tiring: "The rejection of all false irenicism is for me an excellent basis from which to start the dialogue of the future. For I consider that the greatest present danger for ecumenism lies in the tendency to dissimulate what separates us, particularly when we meet one another among Christians who are said to be 'open to dialogue'. Since ecumenism has become fashionable there exists on both sides the dangerous temptation to consider discussions in which the partners shift the emphasis in the presentation of their own point of view to make it more acceptable as showing a particularly ecumenical spirit. In fact, this shifting, however slight, often contorts the truth, creates illusions, and so does damage to the cause of ecumenism, because sooner or later it will run into a major deception. The present Decree, while showing a great effort to understand our belief, does not fall into that trap. . . ." The same author hopes that every non-Catholic Church will work out, "on the lines of the Decree, a text that will offer its own principles on ecumenism. . . . Such a confrontation would be extremely fruitful".

(f) *Priorities in Dogma.* According to O. Cullmann, "the most revolutionary passage, not only in the schema *De Oecumenismo,* but in all the conciliar texts" is that which reminds Catholic theologians "that there exists an order or hierarchy of the truths of Catholic teaching, since they differ in their connection with basic Christian belief". This allows them to put such dogmas as the papal primacy and the assumption of Mary no longer on the same level as those that relate to Christ and the Trinity. Here Prof. Cullmann sees "the starting point of ecumenical developments which make it possible to hope everything". Roux and Bonino share the same opinion. In a moving address given before an audience of cardinals and bishops on November 12 at Saint-Louis-des-Français, Pastor Marc Boegner enthusiastically underlined the same idea.

(g) *The "Continuous Reform".* No one has failed to notice the dynamic character of the theology of the Decree. According to H. Roux, the most promising element is the recognition that there is a distance between the essence of the Church and her historical dynamism, and that the search for unity becomes inseparable from a "permanent reform". It is the general opinion that this distinction may lead a long way. Those familiar with the work of

Abbé Couturier, the Bishop of Bristol among them, admire the way in which the text insists on an "interior and continuous reform" and on the "golden rules" of Chapter II: in short, the teaching of a spiritual ecumenism which comes out so splendidly in the Decree. This has been mentioned by Oliver Tomkins and R. McAfee Brown. J. R. Chandran, more involved in missionary problems, points to the common action of all Christians in the underdeveloped world, with reference to the noble expression "that the image of Christ the servant may thus be manifest".

3. *Criticism, Doubts and Ambiguities*

Having gathered so many favorable and even "revolutionary" signs in the course of their reading of the Decree, are the non-Catholic commentators wholly satisfied that the ecumenical enterprise, of which the Decree means to be the Roman Catholic charter, is wholly genuine? We cannot say that, and we feel that they *all* hesitate in their final conclusion. Are they sure they have understood? Are they not victims of an illusion? Is it probable that all 2,137 bishops (against only seven) meant to give a true ecumenical sense to the Decree by giving their *placet*, particularly since so few of them were prepared for it? One does not grow ecumenical wings simply by sitting side by side in a council. Maturity is required, and this means time and practice. Did the bishops yield perhaps to a kind of collective psychosis, and will all this again prove to be another Trojan horse?

That even the most open-minded observers show some hesitation will not astonish those who lived through the last days of the third session. It will be remembered that a crisis[8] was provoked

[8] On the crisis during the last days before the vote, see the studies already quoted. See also some general studies on the third session: R. Laurentin, *L'enjeu du Concile, bilan de la troisième session* (Paris: Ed. du Seuil, 1965), esp. Ch. XVII, "Les surprises des derniers jours," pp. 253-86; A. Wenger, *Vatican II, chronique de la troisième session* (Paris: Centurion, 1965), esp. Ch. XVI, "Le décret sur l'oecuménisme," pp. 303-15; R. Rouquette, "Les derniers jours de la 3e session," in *Etudes* (April, 1965), pp. 556-70; M. Villain, *op. cit.*, pp. 287-92; "Où en est l'oecuménisme? Ne pas désespérer du dialogue," in *Le Figaro* (Dec. 18, 1964); G. Richard-Molard, "Une douleur partagée," in *Réforme* (Nov. 28,

by four incidents: the "explanatory note" to the *Constitution on the Church,* the introduction at the last moment of 19 *modi* to the text of the Decree, the adjournment of the vote on the schema on religious liberty, and the proclamation of Mary as Mother of the Church. It is generally thought today that extreme fatigue made the witnesses of these incidents exaggerate their importance to the detriment of ecumenism, and this opinion is based on more complete information. Nevertheless, during the session the uneasiness increased very considerably, and at the time I write these lines (Pentecost, 1965), an interdenominational meeting of observers and *periti* proved to me that it had not been completely dispelled. And so, our non-Roman brethren can hardly hide their hesitation, and they explain it frankly in the articles I have quoted. I am leaving the details on one side in order to deal at once with the major and, so to speak, the unique and essential obstacle.

They ask whether it is possible that the Roman Church, whatever assurances she may give, is in a condition to inaugurate a dialogue with other Churches as between equals? What, indeed, is meant by ecumenical dialogue in the full sense of that term? It is not a casual meeting for the exchange of amiable platitudes:

1964); J. Crootaers, "Le Concile et le Pape après une session mouvementée," in *De Maand* (Jan., 1965), pp. 16-35; G. Vallquist (Swede), "Vatican II vu de la 60e latitude Nord," in De Maand (end of Feb., 1965), pp. 84-7.

These studies on the whole deal courageously with the facts and are well documented; they reproduce correctly the impression of discouragement that was felt throughout the last week, while admitting that fatigue and nervous strain helped to dampen the atmosphere. Caprile's article adds some details not known at that time, which helped to reassure the general feeling. In this survey I am not going into any detail about this painful affair because the memory gets blunted and in actual fact not everything had to be done all over again. At the time of writing I am glad that the *Decree on Religious Liberty* has been referred to the following session which has brought about a better text. There is far from the same objectivity in the attitude of P. Johnson, an English Catholic, who expressed his disappointment in irritating and irreverent terms ("Chaos au Vatican," in *Nouvel Observateur* of Nov. 19, 1964). Fr. Hillig also points out that, on the whole, the German press has only concentrated on the negative aspects of that crisis ("Das Ergebnis des dritten Konzilsperiode im Spiegel des deutschen Press," in *Stimmen der Zeit,* January, 1965).

the ecumenical smile is but a fire of straw that leaves only bitter disappointments behind. It is not merely a matter of getting to know each other better, of recognizing one another for what one is with the thought at the back of our mind that we are nevertheless right in spite of everything. The ecumenism of confrontation soon touches its limits when it is not turned into a dialogue of smiles. This does not mean that these first two stages are therefore useless, but they cannot be more than a prelude. True dialogue consists in listening to the questions put by the other with the same intensity and disinterestedness with which we would like him to listen to ours and in allowing each other's position to be put to the test by a clear reference to the demands of Christ in the light of one and the same criterion which must ultimately be Holy Scripture. Only in this way can we hope to start on the road of an ecumenical theology *together,* each with an eye on the position of the other.

Now, it seems that our observers still do not think that the text of the Decree allows this to happen because it is still dominated by the view that Rome is the center. This is how Prof. Jean Bosc expresses it:[9]

"The main reservation seems to me the still too one-sided character of the document. I mean that everything seems to be considered too emphatically from the point of view of the Catholic Church as the *center,* and everything is defined in that light. This is felt particularly in Chapter III. This is devoted to an investigation of the Churches separated from the See of Rome. It treats first of all of the Orthodox Churches, and then of the Churches of the Reformation. The analysis is, no doubt, generous; it clearly tries to bring out all that is positive in those communities. But the values stressed here are those which the Roman Catholic Church herself looks on as part of the Christian and Catholic heritage and which she consequently recognizes as of positive significance in the other denominations. In other words, there is a tendency to look in the other Churches for those elements which correspond to the faith of the Roman Catholic

[9] *Op. cit.,* in *Amitié* (June, 1965), p. 6.

Church. But a genuine ecumenical dialogue presupposes that each partner allows himself to be challenged by the others, that he submits himself to being queried, and this does not come out sufficiently [in the Decree], so it seems to me: it reveals a tendency that is still too definitely centered on Rome."

Apart from a few variations, all of them echo the same charges. Pastor Roux finds confirmation of it in the Encyclical *Ecclesiam suam,* which places the other Churches and communities in concentric circles around the See of Rome. And even if the "policy of return" would be done away with, it is difficult not to ask oneself whether the Council fathers did not implicitly reintroduce it in the intention with which they voted. R. McAfee Brown wonders whether one cannot always put the question of the "return" into brackets as long as the Church of Rome maintains that she is the sole true Church and the only one to possess the form of unity, and whether this thought is not always present at a certain hidden level. One could multiply the quotations, all of which point to the same uneasiness.

III

THE REPORT OF DR. LUKAS VISCHER

It is at this point that Dr. Lukas Vischer's report,[10] given at the Conference of Enugu, must be mentioned. Pastor Vischer was the observer delegated by the World Council of Churches to Vatican Council II; he was the principal liaison officer between the Secretariat of Cardinal Bea and that of Dr. Visser 't Hooft, and for that reason he was commissioned to report on the third session of the Council to the Central Committee of the World Council that met at Enugu in Nigeria, January, 1965. He was very sad when he bade us farewell in Rome on November 21, 1964, deeply affected by the latest developments, and it was feared that his report would be interspersed with severe criticisms which might prejudice the immediate development of the rela-

[10] World Council of Churches, Geneva.

tions between the Vatican and the World Council. Who would blame him? But his report was most objective and, without disguising the obscurities and ambiguities, left the way wide open for a hopeful future.

In this very objective report Lukas Vischer mentioned the "struggle", the "violent conflicts" that marked the third session in order to come to concrete conclusions, and there, he said, lies the "greatness" of this session. Like Pastor Richard-Molard, he was not astonished that the Council had to pass through the winter before it could reap the harvest: in other words, through the death of the cross before it could come to the resurrection; but this will also have to be *the fate of all the Churches* on their way to unity, and Vischer invited them *all* to play their part in this painful drama.

He lucidly analyzed the various acts of the Council, particularly the two great texts on the Church and on Ecumenism:

"The results reflect the image of Janus, the god of the doorways, and show two faces. On the one hand, they open the door not only to a renewal in depth, but also to a more profound communion with the Churches separated from Rome. On the other hand, they continue the tradition specific to the Roman Catholic Church; they represent an adaptation of the old Roman Catholic position to this modern age, a transposition in a modern context. All will depend, therefore, on the way in which the texts will be interpreted in the years to come, on that face of Janus to which the Catholic Church will attach herself."

At the moment both interpretations are possible. In the *Constitution on the Church* there seems to be a conflict between the first two chapters, that on the "Mystery of the Church" and that on the "People of God", remarkable for their new outlook, as opposed to the third chapter on "episcopal collegiality", so disturbing for the non-Catholic reader. This third chapter—especially in the light of its "explanatory note" (fortunately left ambiguous)—rather gives the impression that it strengthens the absolutism of Vatican Council I by providing the primacy with a better organic foundation (the college of bishops) instead of balancing it by a genuine collegial formula for the government of the universal Church. This is at least the opinion of a Protestant like Vischer or of an Orthodox like Prof. N. Nissiotis. How could these conditions turn Vatican Council II into a stage further on the way to an "ecclesiology of communion"? One cannot quite see it yet. Insofar as the *Decree on Ecumenism* is concerned, Vischer certainly welcomed the far-reaching improvements on the first draft, but he still strongly resented the centralism of Rome, and his objections of the year before had not been overcome. But I feel, nevertheless, that at this crucial point the observer from Geneva must have realized what importance would be attached to his final judgment before the Central Committee. Was it to be favorable or not? He held in his hands the immediate future of ecumenism. Let us give him credit: he has delivered this judgment in all fairness and greatness.

On examining the work of the third session, he concludes, we end up with a "confused picture"; the results do not reveal a clear tendency and too many questions are left undecided. "The Church of Rome herself is not very clear as to what has happened to her in this Council; the great lines are still but a sketch", and it is impossible to be sure that the possibilities which one can discern here and there will be translated into action.

In these circumstances all Christian Churches must realize that they have a collective responsibility toward the Church of Rome because they are already in communion with her, whether they like it or not:

"This situation provides no justification for an attitude of distant neutrality or of secret malicious satisfaction. . . . The non-Roman Churches must, therefore, be aware of a responsibility. *They must try to develop whatever is still in the state of potentiality in the Council* by collaborating.[11] The expectations of the next stage rest on the dialogue and encounter, based on the sincere confession of the truth. An attitude of withdrawal into themselves would be the surest way of paralyzing the movement started by the Council."

The theologian of Geneva develops this key idea to which the Decree has not yet given the answer: the idea of a "community of

[11] Italics are mine.

dialogue and collaboration among the Churches" with the co-operation of the Church of Rome. It is not enough to repeat the word "dialogue"; it is the contents that matter, and he suggests:

"Could we not examine together what we mean by 'ecumenical relations' and what form we think they should take? Should we not examine our thought about the principles of religious liberty? Should we not try to find a solution for the complex question of proselytism? Should we not begin by asking ourselves how far and in what way separated Churches can provide a common witness, undertake a common action without conflicting with each other in the process? The task to be undertaken here is over-whelming, and the road toward a genuine ecumenical com-munion may seem so uncertain and perilous that one hesitates to commit oneself. But if we do want to achieve that, the obstacle would lie in the non-Roman Churches, because the Roman Catholic Church has resolutely committed herself to the ecumeni-cal dialogue. We cannot arrive at a clarification of this basic disposition if we do not take her seriously and give her an answer."

In conclusion, Dr. Vischer takes up the question of confidence. The World Council has to play a role in this dialogue; it must give the Church of Rome the benefit of its long experience of an ecumenical community and of problems that have already been solved. And so, the moment has come for it to propose *a be-ginning of collaboration* in answer to the Decree, in spite of its ambiguities, without prejudice, of course, to the particular con-versations that each Church could and should undertake to clarify its own situation.

Thus pleaded Dr. Vischer at the Conference of Enugu. Dr. Visser 't Hooft had already expressed similar ideas in his inau-gural report.[12] The decision was taken to set up a "mixed work-ing group" for the study of the principles and method of collab-orating with the Church of Rome.[13] This was a major event in

[12] *Report of the General Secretary to the Central Committee, Enugu, Nigeria* (Jan., 1965), par. 4: "Relations with the Roman Catholic Church," in *Ecumenical Review* (April, 1965), pp. 169-70.

[13] "Relations between the World Council of Churches and the Roman

the history of ecumenism. We know the rest. In this group, which started work at Bossey in June, 1965, the World Council is represented by eight members and the Church of Rome by six. The difference in number is due to the desire that the World Council should represent as fairly as possible the various traditions of its member Churches (Protestant, Anglican, Orthodox and Old Catholic). The program contains those general questions that the World Council as such is competent to deal with: namely, collaboration in Christian action (underdeveloped countries, social and international affairs), participation in theological work on Faith and Order, everything that creates tensions among the Churches (mixed marriages, religious liberty, proselytism), and, finally, everything that concerns the Christian life and the mission of the Church. Reservation is made for other conversations on more special programs between the Church of Rome and those member-Churches of the World Council who wish to take advantage of this.

Rome's reply was favorable.[14] Cardinal Bea took it to Geneva when he paid his memorable visit to the World Council on February 18, 1965, in the company of Pastor Marc Boegner. The report notes that this encounter "bears witness to the putting into practice of the conciliar *Decree on Ecumenism* at the highest level and to the start of a dialogue on equal footing, not centered on Rome, Geneva or Constantinople, but on the person and the work of Christ, based on Holy Scripture in truth and charity, and directed by the Holy Spirit toward such unity as Christ wills and by the means he wills it to the glory of the Father".

May the Spirit bring about that these official conversations, so promisingly started, lead to a riper understanding of the Decree with all its implications and needs so that the labor of ecumenism may truly flourish.

Catholic Church" (Statement adopted by the Central Committee at Enugu), *ibid.*, pp. 171-3.

[14] *Rencontre oecuménique à Genève*. Addresses by Cardinal Bea, Pastor Boegner, Dr. Visser 't Hooft, Prof. N. Nissiotis and Prof. O. Cullmann. *Collection oecuménique*, n. 4 (Labor et Fides, 1965).

Hilaire Marot, O.S.B./*Chevetogne, Belgium*

Decrees of Vatican II:
First Orthodox Reactions

The first few and as yet incomplete Orthodox reactions to Vatican Council II are interesting. They converge largely upon the same issues, particularly on the question of the Roman primacy and its effects on ecclesiology. In addition, these reactions reveal new points of view distinct from the usual "conservative" and "progressive" positions; moreover, in the "progressive" camp a certain inner conflict in the new "eucharistic" ecclesiology is evident, and we shall discuss this in the course of our presentation. In speaking of the Council, then, we can point to a new fermentation that promises many rewards for future dialogue.

I

THE CONSTITUTION ON THE CHURCH AND GREEK THEOLOGY

1. *A Conservative Reaction*

M. J. Karmiris, Professor at the University of Athens, has published a series of highly informative articles on the texts promulgated at the Council's third session. They appeared in *Ekklesia,*[1] the official journal of the Greek Church. These articles

---

[1] M. Karmiris, "Hē y' phasis tēs B' Batikaneiou Synodou," in *Ekklēsia* 42 (1965). On the *Constitution on the Church,* see pp. 221-5, 251-4, 309-

were valuable because they put at the disposal of Greek theologians extensive quotations from the most important passages of
the Decrees. With regard to the *Constitution on the Church,*
Karmiris' criticism was centered only on Chapter III (on the
hierarchy) and Chapter VIII (on the Blessed Virgin); the other
chapters seemed to meet with his unqualified approval.[2] In his
discussion of mariology,[3] he rejected those titles of the Virgin
whose scope and meaning are disputed among Catholics and
which were not taken up at the Council; he was especially critical
of the dogma of the immaculate conception and the dogma of the
assumption. Furthermore, he disapproved of proclaiming Mary
"Mater Ecclesiae" (Mother of the Church), asserting that it had
widened the breach between the two Churches.

Karmiris contends that Eastern veneration of the Mother of
God in the liturgy and in sometimes profound pious devotions
has not had the same effect on Orthodox dogma as on Roman.
But for him and for other Orthodox Churchmen, Chapter III
demands close attention.[4] Though he is rather selective in his
choice of facts, his commentary is for that reason all the more re-
warding.

Admittedly, the *Constitution on the Church* rarely mentions
the bishops without affirming the papal prerogatives set down at
Vatican Council I in a defensive and apprehensive state of mind.
Karmiris cites those passages which cause most difficulty for the
Orthodox, ignoring other passages where such problems are met
more satisfactorily.

As a conservative, he readily admits the notion of episcopal
collegiality in itself, but the emphasis in Chapter III upon the
primacy partly conceals from him the real position of the Council.

13, 334-40, 356-63, 390-97. On this topic cf. the brief study by F. van
de Paverd, "Eine Griechisch-Orthodoxe Reaktion auf die 3 Session des
Vatikanum II," in *Ostkirchliche Studien* 14 (1965), pp. 203-12, especially pp. 207ff.

[2] In connection with the quasi-identification of the Church with the
Roman Catholic Church, M. Karmiris refers to a sprightly critique by
G. Stathis in *Kathēmerinē* (May 18, 1965).

[3] Karmiris, *op. cit.*, pp. 359-63.

[4] *Ibid.*, pp. 334-40.

Thus, reasoning from the fact of the necessity of hierarchical communion with the pope and the necessity of his intervention in the
acts of the episcopal college, he concludes that the powers of the
college are derived from those of the pope. "The college is absolutely dependent on the pope; it is merely the shadow cast by
the fullness of papal power; it is a body receiving its light, power
and authority from the sole source of light and power, the pope."
Consequently, Karmiris contends that Vatican Council II seems
to have reinforced the teachings of Vatican Council I.[5]

In interpreting these positions taken at the Council, Karmiris
presents an outline of the Orthodox teaching as well, in the hope
of setting the theological dialogue in perspective.[6] His ecclesiology
is the traditional Orthodox teaching, uninfluenced by the *Sobornost* (of Russian origin). This doctrine tends to minimize the
role of the hierarchy and to stress the importance of all the
People of God.[7] It is with this relationship in mind that Karmiris
approaches Chapter III of the *Constitution on the Church*.

Indeed, according to Karmiris, in the synodal system of the
ancient Church "the assembly of all the bishops reunited in the
same place constituted the common, collegial power of the
Church". The ecumenical council, insofar as it was the reunion of
all the bishops, the successors of the apostles, had the supreme
power of government, and in its unity "reflected the unity of the
persons of the Trinity".

The council forms its teachings under the inspiration of the
Holy Spirit, and thus its dogmatic decrees are infallible and constitute the basic teaching of the Church. But no bishop possesses
in his own person the fullness of ecclesiastical power; all the
bishops are, by divine right, absolutely equal. This excludes the
possibility of any universal primacy exercising its sovereign right
over an ecumenical council or over the bishops dispersed through-

---

[5] *Ibid.*, pp. 337-8.
[6] *Ibid.*, pp. 339-40.
[7] *Sobornost* signifies "conciliarity" (*conciliarité*), and it is currently
used with reference to the teachings of the Russian theologian, Khomiakov
(1804-1860), who had a profound influence on Orthodox theology.

out the world: in short, over any "particular", "collegial" or, especially, any "conciliar" authority.

Thus the Petrine primacy, "subsequently introduced by the Latin Church", a primacy which both Vatican Council I and Vatican Council II treated in their dogmatic pronouncements, is considered "a secular innovation". Furthermore, Karmiris seems unable to envision, in connection with a renewed view of history, a mitigated form of primacy (proposed by other Orthodox theologians whom we shall discuss later) that would be more acceptable to the Orthodox Church.

In summary, we may say that his comments are the kind of traditional reaction on the part of Orthodox conservative theology that continues to be predominant in Greek thought.[8] In addition, Karmiris' frankly negative position on the points mentioned does not seem to be without value, for he himself alludes to the possibility of worthwhile dialogue.

2. A Progressive Reaction

Nikos Nissiotis, Director of the Ecumenical Institute at Bossey and an Observer at Vatican Council II, is one of the representatives of the "progressive" tendency in Orthodox thought, and thus he fully adheres to the *Sobornost;* he evaluates the *Constitution on the Church* in the light of this "conciliarity of the entire Church".

He presents his point of view in an article entitled "The Main Ecclesiological Problems of Vatican II".[9] Here certain elements, borrowed from the Russian theology of the Institut St. Serge (Paris), are reviewed in a personal synthesis which may have a

[8] Especially in the work of M. P. Trembelas, author of an important dogmatic treatise.

[9] Nikos Nissiotis, "The Main Ecclesiological Problem of the Second Vatican Council and the Position of the Non-Roman Churches Facing It," in *Journal of Ecumenical Studies* 2 (Winter, 1965), pp. 31-62. There is a résumé of this article, entitled "Ecclesiology at Vatican II," in *Herder Correspondence* 2 (1964-1965), pp. 272-7. Nissiotis has himself recently revised this article in large part in "Okumenische Bewegung und zweites Vatikanisches Konzil," in *Kerygma und Dogma* 11 (1965), pp. 208-19.

slight tendency to force some parts to fit a pattern. Nissiotis maintains that Chapter III, whose juridicism has repercussions on the rest of the Constitution, appears to have no apparent connection with the first two satisfactory chapters on the Church as mystery and on the People of God.

He reduces his criticism to three interrelated main points: (1) an apostolicity, limited to the episcopate; (2) collegiality, considered apart from the *pleroma* (fullness) of the Church; and, above all, (3) defects in the theology of the Holy Spirit (pneumatology).

1. In the first place, the Western Church has always been more concerned with the passing on of Christ's authority than with the action of the Holy Spirit. The latter has been the main concern of the Eastern Church. Thus, Western thought on the direct succession (Christ/apostles/bishops) has not taken enough account of the intervention of the pentecostal event, without which the full reality of the *Ecclesia* cannot be understood.[10] Thus, beyond the simple kind of "priority" admitted by the Orthodox Church,[11] the Petrine primacy has undergone a development to the point of being the sole, ultimate guarantee of apostolicity. "This identity of the Bishop of Rome with Peter does not mean that he is simply Peter's successor, but that the supreme right of guidance and authority which Peter had over the other apostles, the pope has over the other bishops."

Vatican Council II has tried to reestablish a balance by referring to the eleven-united-to-Peter whose successors are the bishops: "The one line—Christ/Peter/popes—of Vatican Council I is now completed by the second—Christ/eleven apostles/bishops. . . . Vatican Council II does not alter the line of Vatican Council I but extends the divine right to all bishops, yet placing their authority under the pope's absolute authority." Hence, there is a continual and unchanged reaffirmation of the

---

[10] Nissiotis, *op. cit.*, p. 40.

[11] Cf. N. Afanassieff, N. Koulomzine, J. Meyendorff, A. Schmemann, *La Primauté de Pierre dans l'Eglise Orthodoxe* (Neuchâtel, 1960); Eng. tr.: *Primacy of Peter* (London: Faith Press, 1963).

primacy.[12] "The Orthodox are afraid that the collegiality of the bishops [thus understood] introduces a new deviation into ecclesiology without correcting the monarchical system.[13] The apostolicity of the Church is limited to her hierarchy as the backbone of the Church preserving external juridical order and clothed with authority to govern the subordinate priesthood and the laity."

Faced with this alleged limitation of apostolicity, Nissiotis, in company with other Orthodox theologians, feels constrained to remind us that "the twelve apostles are not to be regarded as 'one plus eleven'. They are together as Twelve with the prophets and martyrs, whose common cornerstone is Christ alone". He further states that there were other apostles besides the Twelve, Paul in particular; that ecclesiastical decisions are binding only when made in common with the presbyters and the entire Church (Acts 15, 22); that the apostolicity of the bishops is that of the Church and not vice versa; that in the People of God the bishops are endowed with the supreme charism of personifying this apostolicity in a distinctive way; and, finally, that a bishop exists in a local community: bishop and Church are correlative.[14]

2. On the second point (collegiality considered apart from the *pleroma* of the *Ecclesia*), Nissiotis regrets that Vatican Council II did not strive to treat collegiality in connection with the fullness of the Church.[15] The episcopacy remains a separate entity, isolated in particular from the laity (whom he identifies with the People of God, *Laos Theou*). "Not only the texts but the Council itself betray an excessive concern to classify the People of God in categories and to make these categories sacred." [16]

[12] Nissiotis, *op. cit.*, p. 42.
[13] *Ibid.*, p. 43.
[14] *Ibid.*, pp. 43-4.
[15] In an article appearing during the second session, Nissiotis had already presented a rather full outline of the same criticisms: cf. "Die Ekklesiologie des zweiten Vatikanischen Konzils in Orthodoxer Sicht," in *Kerygma und Dogma* (1964), pp. 153-68. In it he looked upon collegiality as "a very vague term, entirely devoid of any biblical or historical basis" (p. 157).
[16] Nissiotis, *op. cit.*, p. 46.

Although there exists a hierarchy, the Church is still not to be broken up into different departments. Significantly, Nissiotis comes back to this subject in connection with the primacy. The Orthodox do recognize certain priorities. Following some of these theologians, he affirms that "the priority of Rome, the Apostolic See, the city of martyrs, the capital of the empire", is a "priority of honor, respect and love, a gift of the Holy Spirit to the Church", yet always with respect for the facts of history and the nature of the Church.[17]

"Between the monarchism and the collective authority of episcopacy [Rome and the classical Orthodox teaching], the Orthodox of the East, including the non-Chalcedonian Churches, struggle to maintain the ancient oligarchy for the sake of charismatic unity, where order is structured on the whole People of God, and not on the divine right reserved for one specific place." And yet, the text can open up new avenues toward a decentralization based on national episcopal conferences and on an interpretation of the primacy more acceptable to the non-Roman Churches. This should be the target, he feels, of Orthodox hopes and prayers.[18]

3. The final and basic criticism centers about what Nissiotis considers an almost complete lack of sound pneumatology. We may note, moreover, that this is a sore point in Western tradition in general. Nissiotis sees here a justification for those Orthodox theologians who attach great importance to the *Filioque* issue. Defects in pneumatology lead to "an exaggerated preoccupation with the hierarchical structure", without "sufficient reference to the totality, the whole, the *pleroma* of the Church". This threatens to reduce the unity of the Church to "a matter of discipline and obedience of the less important 'categories of the People of God' to the superior ones".[19]

"The lack of a theology of the Holy Spirit, as the actual

[17] *Ibid.*, p. 47. Cf. above, footnote 11.
[18] *Ibid.*, p. 48.
[19] *Ibid.*, pp. 48-9. Cf., however, the hierarchical order, the *taxis*, so evident in the thought of Clement and especially of Ignatius.

founder of the historical Church . . . allows the intervention of the human institution." In the acts of Vatican Council II, the Spirit is merely "the guarantee of the harmony of the divine and human aspects of the Church, the guarantee of the divine origin of ecclesiastical authority, the guarantee of the harmonious relationship between pope and bishops, hierarchy and laity". Nissiotis is pleased, nonetheless, that in the final text the Holy Spirit is mentioned in four crucial places, and even more pleased that the event of Pentecost is mentioned as "contributing to the realization of the first community of believers". Nevertheless, this does not change that attitude mentioned above, which overlooks the creative role of the Holy Spirit with respect to the body of Christ in its fullness, and especially with respect to teachers, prophets, bishops and charismatic persons.[20]

"Orthodoxy," Nissiotis continues, "does not deny the relationship between the apostolicity of the Twelve and the bishops of the Church in all centuries, but this apostolicity passes through the gathered People of God by the descent of the Holy Spirit on the day of Pentecost." This is the essential point in Nissiotis' summary. It is precisely this failure to mention the Holy Spirit on the day of Pentecost (except in the final text) that led to the inclusion of Chapter VIII on the Blessed Virgin. The doctrinal pronouncements in this chapter cause some confusion between the work of the Holy Spirit as previously explained, and the work of Mary (called "Mater Ecclesiae") as mediatrix in a specific sense distinct from intercession. Nissiotis contrasts Roman dogmatizing in mariology to the limited Orthodox teaching on the *Theotokos,* and the Orthodox "doxological-hymnological" way of worshiping Mary.[21]

Nissiotis summarizes his systematic criticism in these words: "It is possible to speak of the work of the Holy Spirit being subordinated to the work of Christ in the realm of ecclesiology." It might well be that he is to some extent correct, but his posi-

[20] *Ibid.,* p. 49.
[21] *Ibid.,* pp. 50-3.

tion seems to me to lead to another kind of subordination, disrupting a delicate balance between christology and pneumatology.[22]

II

RUSSIAN THEOLOGY AND THE CONSTITUTION ON THE CHURCH

1. *The Constitution as a Whole*

Nicholas Arseniev, a respected figure in Orthodox spiritual theology,[23] has presented a commentary that goes beyond Chapter III. To do full justice to the document, it seems necessary, he feels, to examine it as a whole, for it involves more than the relations between the episcopacy and the papacy. He heartily approves of the general character and tone of the text. He is impressed by its christological quality (which he finds altogether agreeable) and also by its missionary zeal for reaching the contemporary world searching for enlightenment. As far as he is concerned, ecclesiology ought always to be *subordinated to christology*.[24] Thus, the danger of identifying the Church on earth with the kingdom itself is avoided, and this eschatological attitude gives a dynamic quality to the whole presentation. "All this," he says, "is Christian and apostolic and dear to the heart of the Orthodox Church."

The work of the Spirit as it is explained in the section on the

[22] Concerning this issue in recent Orthodox theology, see the article by E. Lanne cited below in footnote 32. With respect to the second session we may point to the article by the young Greek theologian, P. Nellas, "Collégialité une problème nouveau," in *Le Messager Orthodoxe* 24-25 (1964), pp. 12-20; his extreme position seems to question the existence of a hierarchy. The notion of collegiality has been defended in the course of this discussion by the Orthodox theologian, E. Behr-Sigel, in *Contacts* 16 (1964), pp. 238-9. See also P. Nellas, "A Propos de la Collégialité épiscopale," in *Contacts* 17 (1965), pp. 77-80, and E. Behr-Sigel, "Réponse à P. Nellas," *ibid.,* pp. 80-2. P. Nellas is often in agreement with Nissiotis.

[23] Nicholas Arseniev, "The Second Vatican Council's 'Constitutio de Ecclesia,' " in *St. Vladimir's Seminary Quarterly* 9 (1965), pp. 16-25.

[24] Arseniev, *op. cit.,* p. 17 (Arseniev's emphasis).

body of Christ is rightly treated in Pauline terms. Arseniev comments favorably on the passage dealing with the poor and suffering Church, and he notes that the basic profound cause for the recent events within the Church is surely the Church's assertion that there exists a permanent need for self-reform and purification—all this in order to preach the Gospel.[25]

Chapter II on the People of God reveals, he says, the sense of common responsibility of the whole Church, a dynamic conception of the Church guided by the Spirit; this reminds Arseniev—and this is a point of some ecumenical importance—of the beautiful passages dedicated to this subject by the Russian theologian, A. S. Khomiakov, who popularized the *Sobornost* doctrine in the 19th century.[26]

This clarification of episcopal powers suggests certain elements in Orthodox teaching, but here the whole question of the primacy comes in. Arseniev, referring to the key passages "continually repeated", emphasizes that the dogmatic formulas of Vatican Council I have been restated, both on the primacy and on infallibility; and as regards infallibility, nothing whatsoever has been changed. The stress placed, henceforward, on the role of the episcopacy in the Church introduces a note of duality into the teaching on the Church's structure, but it is a duality in unity. This view might seem to be progressing toward the ancient position held by the Orthodox Church, marking a progress in solving the problems of Christian unity.

However, a preliminary note (*nota praevia*) seems to put great emphasis on subordination and centralization, making the full exercise of episcopal powers depend upon the authority of the pope, and this renders problematic a wider collegiality in the Church's life.[27]

Nevertheless, it remains true that there has been remarkable progress. The Council, says Arseniev, "has given utterance with admirable force to the new inspiration of going forth—in hu-

[25] *Ibid.*, pp. 17-8.
[26] *Ibid.*, pp. 19-20.
[27] *Ibid.*, pp. 20-3.

mility and poverty—toward the suffering, unbelieving world, not to condemn it, but *to preach to it the salvation of Christ"*.[28]

2. *Chapter III: A Russian Report*

A. Kazem-Bek has written, as he did for the preceding sessions, a highly informative report on the third session in the Journal of the Moscow Patriarchate.[29] In it he reviews, with some commentary, the main ideas surrounding the 39 preliminary ballots on Chapter III (collegiality). He remarks that "what has been specified as episcopal collegiality expresses in weaker terminology the notion of the *Sobornost* (collegiality) of the bishops in the Church", and that "from the Orthodox point of view the question of episcopal *Sobornost* and of its derivation from apostolic *Sobornost* is of the utmost importance".[30] He approves of the votes that reflect the interpretation of the Orthodox and ancient Church, and he reserves a brief but pointed criticism for the rest.[31]

3. *"Eucharistic Ecclesiology" and the Constitution on the Church*

Two Russian theologians from the Institut St. Serge in Paris have recorded their initial reactions to Chapter III on the hierarchy and the problems surrounding it: N. Afanassieff, a professor at St. Serge, and his disciple, J. Meyendorff, who is now teaching in New York.

With special regard for "eucharistic" theology each man takes a stand on the conciliar document. Afanassieff, it may be recalled, has for some twenty years developed an ecclesiology of the local Church, which he calls "eucharistic". He asserts that the whole Church, the body of Christ, is present in its fullness, especially in the eucharistic celebration, in each local, episcopal

---

[28] *Ibid.,* p. 23.
[29] A. Kazem-Bek, "Posle tretjej sessij II Vatikanskogo sobora, Papa Pavel VI, Kollegialjnostj episcopata i rimskij primat," in *Žurnal Moskovskoj Patriarchij* (1965), pp. 67-79.
[30] *Ibid.,* p. 75.
[31] *Ibid.,* pp. 75-8.

Church.[32] He proposes what Meyendorff has called "one of the most interesting modern attempts to restore the primitive notion of the Church". His theology has even had a judicious influence on the Constitution itself.[33]

Although a broad base of agreement exists between them, there has been a recent (around the time of the publication of the conciliar documents) and rather deep difference of opinion in their thought. Meyendorff hesitates to follow his mentor in the apparently logical conclusions recently expressed by Afanassieff, especially with regard to a totally negative stance vis-à-vis any "universal" element in ecclesiology and—as we shall see with regard to the *Decree on Ecumenism*—Afanassieff's acceptance of *communicatio in sacris*.

4. Nicolas Afanassieff and Collegiality

At a solemn convocation at the Institut St. Serge on March 28, 1965, Afanassieff expressed his views on the *Constitution on the Church* and revealed without equivocation his personal doubts on the issue of collegiality.[34] Speaking from a historical viewpoint, he denied the existence of the apostolic college and the episcopal college. While Christ was living, the apostolic group had no juridical character; afterward there was no trace of a college; the exegetical problems of Acts 15 are well known, and then the apostles were dispersed throughout the world as individuals.

The transition from the apostolic college to the episcopal college cannot be determined. St. Cyprian knew only of local councils. Collegiality should have been quite decidedly uni-

[32] On the subject of eucharistic ecclesiology up to 1964, see Hans-Joachim Schulz, "The Dialogue with the Orthodox," in *Concilium* Vol. 4 (Glen Rock, N.J.: Paulist Press, 1965), pp. 131-49, especially pp. 131-3; cf. also E. Lanne, "Die Kirche als Mysterium und Institution in der orthodoxen Theologie," in F. Holböck and T. Sartory, *Mysterium Kirche* (Salzburg, 1962), pp. 892-925; French tr.: "Le Mystère de l'Eglise dans la perspective de la théologie Orthodoxe," in *Irénikon* 35 (1962), pp. 171-212; cf. also B. Schultze, "Universal or Eucharistic Ecclesiology?" in *Unitas* 17 (1965), pp. 87-106.

[33] At the beginning of the paragraph on the bishop as sanctifier.

[34] N. Afanassieff, "Réflexions d'un orthodoxe sur la collégialité des evêques," in *Le Messager Orthodoxe* 29-30 (1965), pp. 7-15.

versal, and this was not apparent at ecumenical councils since these were only partial gatherings of bishops often at odds with each other. Finally, after the division of the Churches, "we would have to concede", he said, "if we are to talk of collegiality, that there were two colleges struggling against each other". Consequently, the idea of collegiality cannot find any historical basis in fact.[35]

In addition, from an ecclesiological point of view, the notion of authentic apostolic succession excludes collegiality. Afanassieff makes a distinction between "personal" succession (the bishops of a local Church being the successors of a certain apostle) and "collective" succession. The sometimes legendary notion of personal succession[36] is "solidly based in ecclesial consciousness". The collective succession of the apostles (in the Constitution, the bishops in relation to the eleven) is difficult to establish historically and still more so in ("eucharistic") ecclesiology.

Thus Afanassieff opts for the form that he feels is the ancient one: all the bishops equally share the Petrine succession. This is the current interpretation of St. Cyprian's teaching on the *Cathedra Petri,* but Afanassieff changes it by the meaning he attaches to the eucharistic rule of each bishop in his local Church; thus, he makes the collegial form of this succession problematic:[37]

"If one adheres to the teaching on collegiality, it is inevitable that the shaky balance of papacy/episcopacy should lean to the side of the pope; one can no longer speak of the sovereign power of the episcopacy, which belongs only to the pope, and which could, with his consent and in certain instances determined by him, be shared by the episcopal college which ought always to act with the pope's consent."

As for the practical results of collegiality, the papal synod corresponds to the patriarchal synod dear to Orthodoxy, but the limited number of bishops excludes the possibility of any real

[85] Afanassieff, *op. cit.,* pp. 8-9.
[86] The author allows that this is authentic for the Church of Rome.
[87] *Ibid.,* pp. 9-10.

collegiality. In Afanassieff's opinion, the same is true of episcopal conferences and regional councils which are more of a "limitation of the principle of collegiality".[38]

However, in his reluctance to give the impression that his view of collegiality is thoroughly negative, he envisions, in the union of the bishops with the supreme authority, more shepherds rather than administrators of the flock.

The doctrine of collegiality is thus wholly in keeping with a universal ecclesiology that is the common endowment of Orthodoxy and the Catholic Church. The ancient Church formed her teaching not in a universal framework but within the local Church; what transpired in each Church had to be accepted by the other Churches, and in the process of this "acceptance" certain Churches came to play a more important role. With the promulgation of the *Constitution on the Church*, it would seem that we are as yet "far from the teaching of the local Church".

5. John Meyendorff: Toward a Synthesis?

In framing his position on the *Constitution on the Church*,[39] Meyendorff seems to have discovered a *via media*, a middle ground between the ecclesiology expressed in this document and the extreme position of Afanassieff;[40] he agrees with the latter's point of departure—the local Church as the sacramental community, the body of Christ in its fullness. By this both men mean the ecclesiology of St. Cyprian, wherein the head of any local Church possesses, with the *Cathedra Petri*, the Petrine succession. But he does not hesitate to acknowledge that Cyprian "was also the great doctor of episcopal collegiality", even though this is

[38] *Ibid.*, pp. 11-3.

[39] John Meyendorff, "Vatican II, A Preliminary Reaction," in *St. Vladimir's Seminary Quarterly* 9 (1965), pp. 26-37, especially pp. 30-7 on the *Constitution on the Church*.

[40] For a moderate criticism of episcopal collegiality up to the time of the debates at the second session of the Council, cf. J. Meyendorff, "Papauté et Collégialité," in *Le Messager Orthodoxe* 24-25 (1963-1964), pp. 3-7. Cf. also P. L'Huillier, "A propos de la collégialité épiscopale," *ibid.*, pp. 8-12.

connected in Cyprian's thought with "the functional identity of the bishops".[41]

The *Constitution on the Church,* Meyendorff observes, includes a good résumé of the eucharistic ecclesiology of the local Church. But other passages contradict or overlook these ideas, considering the local Churches as "parts" of a "whole", or by treating the relationship of the bishop to the local Church in terms of episcopal functions and not of the origin or nature of the episcopate. The origin of the episcopate is defined exclusively by the doctrine of (collective) apostolic succession, and yet the episcopal office is first of all an inherent function of the local Church both in Eastern and Western tradition.

Meyendorff further notes that there are functions "in a particular community which qualify the bishop to participate in the college of the universal episcopate. Participation in the college is, of course, a necessary element in the function of the bishop and a sign of the authenticity of his episcopacy—the collegial character of episcopal ordination bears witness to this—but it is for his local Church and within its very bosom, confirmed by the communion and witness of all the other Churches, that the episcopate is given to him".[42]

The connection between the "universal" and the "sacramental" rightly seems a crucial problem to Meyendorff, and he strives to find some solution that is not on an exclusively logical or juridical level. He looks for some *via media* between an overly schematized eucharistic ecclesiology (as in Afanassieff), which overlooks the "universal" dimension of the Church, and the ecclesiology of Vatican Council II which, "despite certain appearances to the contrary, has in no way modified an ecclesiology constructed as a function of the universal mission of the Church and not as a function of the Church's sacramental nature". Constant references to the Roman primacy indicate that the ecclesiological character of a particular Church is fully manifested only

---

[41] Meyendorff attributes great importance to St. Cyprian in seeing that there was an ecclesiology common to the ancient Church and the later Byzantine Church.

[42] *Ibid.,* pp. 30-2.

in that unity with the See of Rome which "makes the Church to be the Church".

Meyendorff emphasizes in this context the subordination to the pope of the episcopal college, as well as of the ordinary power of the bishops, by asserting that the Council "does not consider the episcopal office itself as a delegation of papal powers, and yet the *exercise* of the episcopate is still placed in total dependence on the Roman pontiff, and this by divine right".

Collegiality, then, fits into a universal canonical structure. Meyendorff looks for a further balance: "A sound concept of episcopacy presupposes a double representation: the bishop is at *the same time* the man of his particular Church within the universal college, and, by virtue of the apostolic succession in his diocese and of his participation in the college, the representative of God in his Church. If one of the elements of this balance is excluded, there is a fall either into Congregationalism or into a concept of the Church which applies the image of the local community to the universal Church, *i.e.,* a single "universal" bishop surrounded by a college of presbyter-bishops."

Safeguarding the notion of collegiality, Meyendorff urges the Orthodox to recognize that the very existence of a universal college implies a certain structure, indeed a *primus,* whose priority is not necessarily just a primacy of honor. He feels that one weakness may be the absence of any mention of *interdependence* between the pope and the bishops in the texts of Vatican Council II on collegiality, "thereby depriving them of much real value". It is his opinion that, due to the teaching of "universal" ecclesiology, it "was probably out of the question to think that the Council would proclaim such an interdependence".[43]

In looking for this "balance", Meyendorff seems to lean strongly toward the single local Church whose only norm and guide is the Holy Spirit, though he does not directly intend to minimize the importance of the "college of bishops". He concludes, moreover, with the hope that the Constitution will in time lead to many unforeseen developments and "create a real

[43] *Ibid.,* pp. 33-34.

counter-balance to papal supremacy". All this, he asserts, "can perhaps give some practical meaning to what today seems a trifle 'out of context' ". This, I feel, is a point of no little importance. Meyendorff has made a significant initial contribution toward the solution of a crucial problem, the synthesis of "universal" and "eucharistic" ecclesiology that is often too much resisted by theologians. His ideas are an invitation to serious reflection.

III

The Decree on Ecumenism

The Orthodox, it seems to me, have not been too enthusiastic over the *Decree on Ecumenism,* and have perhaps not sufficiently noticed the point of view, so favorable to the Orthodox Church, expressed in the section on the Eastern Churches and commented upon honestly and authoritatively by Cardinal Lercaro.[44] Perhaps this is because of the passage on the Uniat Churches— which really does not belong in this place—or the passage— which is still basically positive—on the question of *communicatio in sacris,* or the place given to Orthodoxy in Chapter I.[45]

1. *Paul Evdokimov and the "Orthodox Tradition"*

M. Karmiris, cited above, has insisted upon the "Romanocentric" character of the entire document.[46] Evdokimov has made

---

[44] Cardinal G. Lercaro, "La signification du Décret *De Oecumenismo* pour le dialogue avec les Eglises Orientales non catholiques," in *Irénikon* 37 (1964), pp. 467-86.

[45] Where the Orthodox Church is discussed together with the other non-Roman Churches.

[46] M. J. Karmiris, in his article in *Ekklēsia* 42 (1965), pp. 391-8, cites almost the entire first chapter of the *Decree on Ecumenism* as well as the section on the Eastern Churches in chapter 3. He remarks: "It is superfluous to point out that much of the argumentation is unacceptable, for it presupposes the Roman Church's own assertion that she alone is the one true Church, while all the others (the Orthodox Church included) have retained only the *Vestigia Ecclesiae.*" At the end of Chapter III, he points to many positive points that may be introduced into the dialogue,

some comments on the question in a collection of brief commentaries that appeared in *The Ecumenical Review*.[47] He praises the text, describing it as "revolutionary". However, he regrets the term "separated brethren" and deplores the insertion of the paragraph on the Uniats (already referred to) as the source of much uncertainty; the decisions on *communicatio in sacris*, he feels, obscure the meaning of the ecclesiological bases by taking premature steps (this serious objection will recur again).[48] He looks for a doctrinal definition of the expression "the non-Roman Churches and ecclesial communities". However, despite the presence of a "Romanocentrism", the text is an invitation to dialogue "on an equal footing". He interprets the expression as an appeal to return to Orthodoxy, which proposes subjection not to any historic, localized Orthodox institution, but—and this should be noted—under an attenuated form "which would transcend the existing institutions".

He does not speak of a reunion with any historic Orthodox institution, but of an acceptance of "Orthodoxy" and of the ecclesial tradition to which the Orthodox Church herself would be amenable. A view recently proposed by A. Schmemann seems to be involved here.[49]

---

but remain severely weakened because of the premises of the Roman Church. On the subject of *communicatio in sacris,* he is forced to point to the strict orders of the ecumenical patriarchate for ecumenical meetings. On the delicate topic of "Romanocentrism", see the article by Karmiris, "Tendenzen hinsichtlich der christlichen Einheit," in *Kyrios* 4 (1964), pp. 241ff.

[47] Cf. also Karmiris, "Comments on the Decree on Ecumenism," in *The Ecumenical Review* 17 (1964-1965), pp. 97-101.

[48] In an article that appeared during the second session, P. Evdokimov, while allowing for the coexistence of two traditions in the East and West, showed himself very open on the question of *communicatio.* Cf. P. Evdokimov, "Communicatio in Sacris: Une possibilité," in *Le Messager Orthodoxe* 24-25 (1963-1964), pp. 27-31.

[49] A. Schmemann, "Unité, séparation, réunion à la lumière de l'ecclésiologie orthodoxe," in *Contacts* 26 (1959), pp. 73-78 (a critique of Afanassieff, "Una Sancta," in *Irénikon* 36 [1963], p. 418). On ecumenical thought up to the beginning of the second session, cf. N. Nissiotis, "Ecclesiology and Ecumenism of the Second Vatican Council," in *The Greek Orthodox Theological Review* 10 (1964), p. 30. Dialogue based on equality is difficult, for Roman ecumenism cannot be separated from

2. *Ecumenism and the Eucharist*

Afanassieff and Meyendorff have reacted to the Decree and especially to the issue of *communicatio in sacris* differently, in terms of their own interpretations of eucharistic ecclesiology outlined above.

Afanassieff. His views on the local Churches as the realization of the fullness of the Church—affected only in appearance by the "divisions" of the Church—allow Afanassieff to maintain a very ecumenical stance with regard to Orthodox-Catholic relations and *communicatio in sacris*. He presents his thoughts in an article that appeared at the close of the debates of the second session.[50]

Despite separation and division, the reality of the Church resides in the eucharist; there is no question of a schism, but only of an interruption in the communion between two local Church groups, each in full possession of ecclesial reality. The restoration of this communion does not necessarily entail the suppression of doctrinal differences, important though they be. He returns briefly to the subject after the third session in an article entitled "L'Eucharistie, principal lien entre catholique et orthodoxe".[51] In summary, he concludes: "This is why the eucharist is not only a bond between the Catholic Church and the Orthodox Church, but is as well the manifestation of the unity of these Churches." This is all part, it seems, of his interpretation of *communicatio in sacris*.

John Meyendorff: Communicatio in Sacris and Roman Ecu-

---

submission to a central geographical-juridical authority. On the subject of "Romanocentrism and Christocentrism" and Orthodoxy "lacking a center", cf. also N. Nissiotis, "Okumenisches Dreikugelspiel?" in *Kirche in der Zeit* 20 (1965), pp. 434-5. On the danger of Orthodoxy beginning in turn to speak of "separated brethren in the West", cf. Nissiotis, "Okumenische Bewegung und zweites Vatikanisches Konzil," in *Kerygma und Dogma* 11 (1965), pp. 208-19, especially p. 218.

[50] N. Afanassieff, "Una Sancta, en mémoire de Jean XXIII, le Pape de l'Amour," in *Irénikon* 36 (1963), pp. 436-75. This article has been strongly criticized by the Greek theologian, P. Trembelas, "Theōriai aparadektoi peri tēn Unam Sanctam," in *Ekklēsia* 41 (1964), pp. 7-13.

[51] *Irénikon* 38 (1965), pp. 337-40.

menism. In the first part of the article outlined above,[52] Meyendorff, discussing the *Decree on Ecumenism,* devotes most of his attention to the question of *communicatio in sacris.* He feels that the way it is handled in the Decree is an illustration of Catholic ecumenism. Afanassieff remains in the background, and Meyendorff rises to the occasion, contesting the former's position as being paradoxically close to that of the Decree.

In effect, Meyendorff interprets *communicatio* as implying some sort of divorce between sacramental and dogmatic truth, a disjunction that he tries to trace to what he feels are two principles of Catholic ecumenism. First, there is a one-sided preoccupation with the Roman primacy as the one decisive factor in the unity of the Church. Under cover of this doctrine, Catholics tend to minimize doctrinal problems while "Orthodox unity is realized only through the community of faith, with Christ and the Holy Spirit as its final criteria".

Secondly, he objects to the assertion in the *Constitution on the Church* of the Catholic Church's "right" to all forms of authentic Christianity, and particularly to valid Orthodox sacraments— sacraments of the "Church"—and what is more, this "right" has an objective value, even though not recognized by non-Catholics. Hence, ecclesiastical authority can in some cases allow the practice of *communicatio* with separated Christians in order to encourage unity.[53] Meyendorff recalls the testimony of Orthodox participants in the ecumenical movement on the principle that *communicatio* can be the sign only of realized unity, the complete unity of life and truth. All theories of "intercommunion", however, presuppose a doctrinal relativism, or a "theological disjunction between the sacramental presence of Christ and his revelation as unique truth".

According to Meyendorff, Catholic ecumenism, though somewhat evasive with regard to the Protestants, encourages "intercommunion" in the case of the Orthodox, and yet the *Constitu-*

[52] Cf. above, footnote 39: "A Preliminary Reaction," pp. 26-9; "Orthodoxie et Catholicité," pp. 138-43.

[53] Ecclesiastical authority does, in fact, include the Orthodox hierarchy.

tion on the Church specifies that Orthodox bishops have no doctrinal authority.[54] The fullness of revelation and sacramental presence are inseparable in the eyes of the Orthodox Church, and yet modern Catholic ecumenism, "with its juridical notion of the Church constructing a universal structure to control and be the guarantee of doctrinal purity, makes a disjunction between sacrament and truth".[55] But he sees this also in the entirely different ecclesiology of Afanassieff, who interprets *communicatio* in another sense. "Even a so-called 'eucharistic' ecclesiology," continues Meyendorff, "can succumb to the same temptation: identifying the Church with the sacramental presence to the point of forgetting what this presence implies. Thus we can see a truly paradoxical coincidence, in favor of intercommunion, between a eucharistic 'extremism' such as that of Father Afanassieff, who otherwise represents one of the most interesting modern attempts to restore the primitive notion of the Church, and the ecumenism of Vatican Council II, based as it is on the principle, diametrically opposed to Afanassieff's, of a universal Church exercising her 'right' to all that is authentically Christian wherever it may be found. In each case, but for the opposite reasons, sacramental communion is separated from communion in the truth." [56]

Without question we may justly ask to what extent Meyendorff's comments are true to the insights of Vatican Council II.[57] In any case, this debate within the realm of eucharistic ecclesiology, arising from the *Decree on Ecumenism* and the acts of Vatican Council II in general, cannot help but enhance the new insights that may be the fruit of projected dialogues between Orthodox and Catholic theologians.[58] The same is true of other observations made by our Orthodox brethren.

[54] This question must be determined.
[55] "Orthodoxie et Catholicité," pp. 140-3.
[56] *Ibid.*, p. 144.
[57] Cf. Lercaro, *op. cit.* above, footnote 44, pp. 484-5.
[58] We shall not speak here of the *Decree on the Catholic Churches of the Eastern Rite.* Orthodox reactions, though few, have been very negative. Ecumenical relations since the Decree have been somewhat weakened (for example, at the Third Pan-Orthodox Conference in Rhodes, which preceded the promulgation of the Decree by a few days). The delicate issue of Uniatism must be faced in this whole discussion.

PART III

DOCUMENTATION
CONCILIUM

Office of the Executive Secretary
Nijmegen, Netherlands

EDITORIAL NOTE. The interest shown by the Christian world in the Encyclical *Mysterium Fidei* proves how much the eucharist is the central and vital "Mystery of the Faith" for all those who believe themselves to be the faithful inheritors of the apostolic tradition "received from the Lord" (1 Cor. 11, 23). Among Catholics, the publication of the document has simply intensified the theologians' efforts to arrive at a deeper understanding of this mystery and to present it in language that our age can understand. Inasmuch as anything the Church does today inevitably has ecumenical repercussions, it is important that we allow our non-Catholic brethren to speak of their attitude toward the eucharist and to give us their opinion on the Encyclical. For this reason, the following pages have been given over to Vilmos Vajta, Director of the Theological Department of the Lutheran World Federation (Strasbourg, France) and Metropolitan Emilianos Timiadis, Representative of the Ecumenical Patriarch of Constantinople at the World Council of Churches in Geneva (Switzerland).

Vilmos Vajta/*Strasbourg, France*

Mysterium Fidei:
A Lutheran View

The Encyclical *Mysterium Fidei,* which appeared on the eve of the fourth session, raises questions that refer, first of all, to the understanding of the achievements of the Council, and, secondly, to the ecumenical dialogue among the Churches. I shall attempt to outline these questions.[1]

1. My first question concerns the *fact* of the Encyclical as such. Although it is directed to the universal Church, an encyclical is based upon the sole initiative of the pope. It has its authority not by canon law, but by the veneration due to the papal office. In the dogmatic *Constitution on the Church* Vatican Council II has defined *collegiality* as the main principle. In the future, should not this principle exert an influence upon papal activity, especially upon communications directed to the universal Church? Concretely, this question is concerned with whether encyclicals in the era of episcopal collegiality should reflect the total theological thinking of the Church. Should not a papal encyclical reflect the leading theological trend of Catholic theology? An analysis of the style and content of the present Encyclical could easily show that these consequences of collegiality have not been considered in *Mysterium Fidei.* This fact is even more surprising because

---

[1] The citations from *Mysterium Fidei* are from the *Study-Club Edition,* with commentary by Anthony T. Padavano, published by the Paulist Press (Glen Rock, N.J., 1966).

157

the Encyclical was published in the middle of conciliar work and had a definite relationship to the problems dealt with by this Council.

This Encyclical must be viewed from a different perspective than a document that the Pope might, for instance, publish after the termination of the Council, voicing his opinion on a specific problem of the Church.

It cannot be denied that the publication of the Encyclical at the beginning of the fourth session had a psychological effect. The Council fathers were confronted with a fact that stresses the right of the Pope to issue admonitions with respect to the doctrine and the life of the Church. The Pope's admonitions must have a bearing on the liberty in which the work of the bishops is carried on. Thus, for the future the question arises whether, after the Council, the Pope will take the liberty of publishing texts that do not completely correspond to the theological and ecclesiastical thought expressed by the Council. The publication of the Encyclical in the middle of the work of the Council confused immensely the question of ultimate authority in the Roman Catholic Church for me as an observer at the Council.

2. This general question gains in acuity if the *theme* of the Encyclical is considered. To a high degree an encyclical on the eucharist must affect questions which the promulgated document, the *Constitution on the Sacred Liturgy,* has already treated. The subjects of the Encyclical are, of course, not limited to the same scope; on the contrary, the Encyclical adds important supplements to the conciliar document. At this point, however, the deeply problematical situation becomes apparent. Why did the Pope not refer the problems of the Encyclical to the Council, or at least to the post-conciliar Commission, for deliberation and comment in order to enable a uniform handling of the question? It cannot be true that the Encyclical had been written as a result of the misuses and errors that became apparent in the wake of the *Constitution on the Sacred Liturgy,* as certain circles, for tactical reasons, now argue. The opinions which the Encyclical appears to attack have been current for some years now, and it

is natural for the public to want to know who had voiced them. The denial published in *L'Osservatore Romano* entangled the question still more, since it was misleading. But the main question is to be found elsewhere.

The fact is that there are two documents, one promulgated by the Council and another published by the Pope. Their themes are closely related. The observer at the Council, as well as the Catholic theologian, is thus confronted with the question regarding the relationship of the two texts. Does the Encyclical represent a commentary on the conciliar document? Will the *Constitution on the Sacred Liturgy* have to be explained in the future in the light of this papal document, or will the Constitution retain its specific value beside the Encyclical? Which of them is valid if the two texts show divergencies? Some questions that are now of utmost importance in the Encyclical most likely have purposely not been dealt with in the Constitution of the Council or have even been put aside as unessential issues. Again the question arises: Which of the two documents may be considered as definitive for present-day Catholic doctrine and practice? These questions are extremely important for the future interpretation of the *Constitution on the Sacred Liturgy*.[2]

3. In order to clarify this point, I have to turn to the *content* of the Encyclical. From the point of view of the future ecumenical dialogue, the statements of the Encyclical concerning the doctrinal formulations of the Catholic Church are of primary interest. It warns against certain opinions that create confusion ". . . as if everyone were permitted to consign to oblivion a doctrine already defined by the Church, or else to interpret it in such a way as to weaken the genuine meaning of the words or the recognized force of the concepts involved".[3] This statement must be challenged. It seems to me that defined Catholic doctrine has, by later developments of doctrine, become forgotten

---

[2] Cf. my evaluation of the *Constitution on the Sacred Liturgy:* "Renewal of Worship," in G. Lindbeck (ed.), *Dialog on the Way* (Minneapolis, 1965), pp. 101-28.

[3] *Mysterium Fidei*, n. 10.

and reinterpreted in such a manner that it no longer can har-
monize with the original meaning of the words.

Permit me to give the following two examples of this: (1) The
tridentine doctrine that all sacraments are instituted by Christ
himself has been radically reinterpreted, and is still maintained
only by declaring the Church as a sacrament. This is a speculative
way of deduction and has nothing to do with Trent; (2) The
doctrine of *extra ecclesiam nulla salus* is also radically reinterpreted. There is a completely different meaning given to what
the Church is. Against an institutional-juridical concept, the
spiritual-mystical understanding has been advanced. In different
documents of the Council, doctrinal statements have appeared
which lead almost to the view that believing non-Christians may
also find salvation (*ex voto*) outside of the Church.

A second reference to dogmatic formulas is extremely unfortunate for ecumenical dialogue. The "rule of language" (*reg-
ula loquendi*) and the "dogmatic formulas" (*formulae dog-
maticae*), as defined in the Catholic Church, still seem to be
accorded an external value which cannot be given up. In these
formulas, so it is said, concepts are expressed "that are not tied
to a certain form of human culture, or to a specific phase of
scientific progress, or to one or other theological school. No,
these formulas present that part of reality which necessary and
universal experience permits the human mind to grasp and to
manifest with apt and exact terms taken from either common or
polished language. For this reason, these formulas are adapted to
men of all times and all places".[4] I wonder if this manner of
speaking is in harmony with the original intention of Pope John
XXIII who prescribed that the Council attempt to accommodate
the doctrines—without changing their content—to the present
time.[5] To defend *formulas* as suitable forever, and thus unchange-
able, seems to hinder an ecumenical dialogue. The purpose of an
ecumenical dialogue could justly be described as an attempt to

[4] *Ibid.*, n. 24.
[5] Pope John's opening address of the Council, October 11, 1962, in
L'Osservatore Romano (October 12, 1962).

find either the same faith behind different terminologies, or to find new understanding of a common faith in terminologies that have not yet been used but can be adequate enough for arriving at a consensus.

Let us now turn to questions in which the relationship of *Mysterium Fidei* to the *Constitution on the Sacred Liturgy* can be examined. The Encyclical rightly points to the fact that the main concern of the *Constitution on the Sacred Liturgy* was its insistence upon the active participation (*actuosa participatio*) of the believers in the liturgy. Although this is acknowledged, the Encyclical very quickly departs from this view of the liturgy. Its insistence upon the private Masses, the doctrine of transubstantiation and the so-called eucharistic cult of the reserved sacrament can be taken as proof of that.

(a) *The Private Mass.* One of the purposes of the Encyclical is to guard the existence of the private Mass.[6] The communal Mass is so highly esteemed, the Encyclical says, that the private Mass is derogated. Therefore, one passage[7] deals especially with the question. Reference is made to the Constitution in the following way: "We should also mention 'the public and social nature of every Mass', a conclusion which clearly follows from the doctrine we have been discussing."[8] This is, to say the least, a strange way of quoting a conciliar document. The text in the *Constitution on the Sacred Liturgy* reads as follows:

"Liturgical services are not private functions, but are celebrations of the Church, which is the 'sacrament of unity', namely, the holy people united and ordered under their bishops.

"Therefore, liturgical services pertain to the whole body of the Church; they manifest it and have effects upon it; but they concern the individual members of the Church in different ways, according to their differing rank, office and actual participation.

"It is to be stressed that whenever rites, according to their specific nature, make provision for communal celebration involv-

[6] *Mysterium Fidei*, n. 11.
[7] *Ibid.*, nn. 32ff.
[8] *Ibid.*, n. 32.

ing the presence and active participation of the faithful, this way of celebrating them is to be preferred, so far as possible, to a celebration that is individual and quasi-private." [9]

In this context, the emphasis is placed upon the communal character of every liturgical act, especially that of the Mass. The minor point concerning the public and social nature of any Mass has been granted a major emphasis. Those present during the sessions when the schema on the liturgy was discussed will remember that this sentence, now made the starting point of the argument, was a later addition in order to avoid the fears of three (!) bishops who saw in this an implied censure for the private Mass. In this situation an allusion to Trent (Denz. 944) was necessary. The emphasis of the tridentine text upon the *communal* nature of the *private* Mass is an argument pressed to the utmost limit of theological speculation. The importance of the Constitution was to make the communal Mass the starting point of the liturgical reflection—to accept the private Mass as a still possible minimum. On the other hand, the Encyclical turns back to argue that the private Mass is the basic truth.

It is a serious question whether at this point the papal Encyclical is in agreement with the conciliar document. Naturally, no one should be naïve enough to think that the conciliar document made private Mass impossible. Nevertheless, the discussion in the Council made some emphases in the final document understandable. The Constitution did not act *against* the private Masses but *for* the communal ones. This was its primary emphasis, which for an observer was of great importance. A biblical and patristic tradition has thereby rightfully been accepted again in the Roman Catholic Church. Does the Encyclical intend to hinder this development?

The value of the private Mass in itself is so highly praised that not one word is said about the *faith* in the high-priestly sacrifice of Christ, which is the sole salvation of mankind. Instead, it

---

[9] *Constitution on the Sacred Liturgy* (Glen Rock, N.J.: Paulist Press, 1964), nn. 26-27.

seems that the mere performance of the private Mass is esteemed so highly that—even without the active participation of the faithful—it contributes more to the salvation of mankind than the use of the sacrament in faithful communion. At least, this is said directly about the priest as a communicant. By his celebration of the private Mass "an abundant treasure of special salutary graces enriches the celebrant, the faithful, the whole Church and the entire world—graces not imparted in the same abundance by the mere reception of holy communion".[10]

If there was an attempt at *pastoralis sollicitudo* and *anxietas* in this Encyclical, the aspect of the reception of the sacrament by the faithful should not be missed. At this point the Constitution seemed to go in a different direction: it focused all interest on the communal Mass. The Encyclical returns to the absolute value of the private Mass. Such a development by no means reflects contemporary Catholic theological scholarship. I dare to suggest that if the Encyclical had been presented as a schema to the Council, it would have been considerably revised at this point. In actuality, it passed unchallenged as authoritative Catholic doctrine promulgated by the pope himself. One-sided ontological thinking is thereby claiming the authority of normative Catholic faith.

(b) This can be proved also from the position taken concerning *the doctrine on the real presence.* This is defined as "real" and "substantial presence": "This presence is called 'real'—by which it is not intended to exclude all other types of presence as if they could not be 'real' too, but because it is presence in the fullest sense: that is, it is a substantial presence by which Christ, the God-Man, is wholly and entirely present. It would therefore be wrong to explain this presence by having recourse to the 'spiritual' nature, as it is called, of the glorified body of Christ, which is present everywhere, or by reducing it to a kind of symbolism, as if this most august sacrament consisted of nothing else than an efficacious sign 'of the spiritual presence of Christ and

[10] *Mysterium Fidei,* n. 32.

of his intimate union with the faithful, members of his mystical body.' " [11]

Later on this presence is defined as "a new 'reality' which we may justly term *ontological*".[12] Against new terminological suggestions such as transignification and transfinalization, the reference to the ontological reality is presented as the safeguard of orthodoxy. The other terms are judged unsatisfactory and one-sided.

In both cases one can ask the question whether the opinions here rejected have been correctly understood. Are not the condemned opinions instead legitimate guards of an isolated ontology which has no existential realization in the body of Christ, creating faith in which the virtue of the cross is solely applied for the salvation of mankind? Where this faith is *not* created, the ontological presence of Christ is for condemnation and death, *i.e.*, is a real presence. This is biblically evident.

It has often been said that the reaction of the Roman Catholic Church to the Reformation has bound her to positions that were one-sided—though legitimate—and hindered her from accepting the fullness of the universal faith of the Church. I am afraid that the Encyclical has not been freed from such an attitude and that it fights against opinions that do not deny the eucharistic reality but claim the necessity of its existential realization in the body of the faithful. The crucial question for this Encyclical from the biblical point of view is whether it is in essential agreement with 1 Corinthians 10, 16-17.

All this means, however, that the aspect of *participation* (*koinonía*), so clearly emphasized in the *Constitution on the Sacred Liturgy*, has appeared only marginally in the Encyclical, having been replaced by a static Scholastic view. Again, there is so much eagerness to guard the presence effected by transubstantiation that the real spiritual effect of this presence is neglected, a tendency which ruled the late Middle Ages and spoiled the communal aspect of the Mass. Has not the Encyclical too quickly in-

---

[11] *Ibid.*, n. 39.
[12] *Ibid.*, n. 46.

tervened in order that the Constitution and its participation-emphasis will have little hope of realization?

(c) *The eucharistic cult* easily corresponds to such a view. In the Encyclical the evidence of the Fathers is used to show how the faithful took the eucharist home with them. To regard this as the same faith which created the Feast of *Corpus Christi* is not only anachronistic but also directly misleading. The purpose of taking home the eucharistic bread was to give it to those who could not come to the liturgy of the congregation. Thus, the bread was consecrated with the purpose of being eaten and not to be preserved, exhibited and adored. To claim the direct continuity of this custom with later developments in the Western Church is impossible, and so too is seeing this "faith" as "loyal to the Word of Christ and of the apostles".[13]

To bind the whole piety of the Christian to the eucharist is of limited merit. It has the following consequences:

1. The real presence of Christ *outside* of the Mass is disregarded,[14] or, more concretely: (a) the sacrament of baptism is completely losing its importance as the eschatological event which is realized in daily mortification and vivification. The sacrament of thanksgiving (eucharist!) for redemption is realistic only in this background; (b) the Word of God is losing its daily impact as God's conversation with mankind.[15]

2. The eucharistic presence is extended beyond the liturgical use: (a) the eucharistic cult leads man into institutions which detract from the institution of the Lord (communion Mass!); (b) the *reserved* sacrament becomes the requirement for the churches and oratories as the "spiritual center of a religious community or of a parish, yes, of the universal Church and of all of humanity, since beneath the appearance of the species, Christ is

---

[13] *Ibid.*, n. 64.

[14] No consequences of the presence of Christ as outlined earlier in the Encyclical (n. 34) are drawn for the Christian's piety. Here the eucharist seems to dominate.

[15] The emphasis on the Word of God is a dominating feature in the *Constitution on the Sacred Liturgy*. Cf., for example, nn. 7, 24, 51ff., and *passim*.

contained, the invisible Head of the Church, the Redeemer of the world, the Center of all hearts, 'by whom all things are and by whom we exist' ".[16] What a contrast to the Constitution (n. 10) where the liturgy of the worshiping Church, especially the eucharist, is regarded as the *"culmen"* and *"fons"* from which grace flows.[17]

The eucharist as communion of the faithful with the Lord and with each other is certainly "the sign and the cause of the unity".[18] The Roman Catholic Church should not forget, how-ever, that the so-called "eucharistic cult" of the reserved sacra-ment is a great obstacle to unity, not only with the separated sons of the Reformation, but also with the East. For this reason, the question can at least be raised concerning the future of the Encyclical, issued so soon after the promulgation of the Con-stitution, which was received by many as a promising sign of *rapprochement* among "all those who in every place call on the name of our Lord Jesus Christ" (1 Cor. 1, 2).

The future will show whether this Encyclical will function as a brake within the Roman Catholic Church and as a hindrance in the ecumenical dialogue. Since the Encyclical is giving such great emphasis to the desire for unity,[19] it is necessary to state frankly that the Encyclical itself has made unity, on the basis of the emphasis given in its text, very difficult. The Oriental Churches may answer for themselves whether the faith expressed in the Encyclical is also theirs, as the Pope hopefully states. For the reasons stated above, it is, at least at some essential points, not the biblically evidenced faith of the universal Church.

[16] *Mysterium Fidei*, n. 68.

[17] Adoration of the reserved sacrament is to be classified according to the Constitution as *"pia exercitia"*, as in *Mediator Dei* (n. 13).

[18] *Mysterium Fidei*, n. 70.

[19] *Ibid.*, n. 73.

Metropolitan Emilianos Timiadis/*Geneva, Switzerland*

Mysterium Fidei:
An Orthodox View

The Encyclical *Mysterium Fidei* has a bearing on both the *Constitution on the Sacred Liturgy* (promulgated on December 4, 1963) and, to a lesser degree, the *Constitution on the Church* (promulgated on November 21, 1964). It does not only ratify them once again but also expects that they will bear abundant fruit through an increase in eucharistic devotion. Nevertheless, the main reason for the Encyclical lies elsewhere. It was motivated by the disquiet, "rather widespread", created by various reactions that did not accord with the line laid down by Rome. It expresses the wish that the hope of a new flourishing of eucharistic piety be not disappointing. There is also the fact that certain avant-garde liturgists have used pejorative expressions with regard to so-called "private" Masses, of which they disapprove. The Pope insists on the importance of the devotion to the consecrated host. The classic argument in favor of this point of view is that Christ, aware of our weakness, desires to remain bodily present among his people under a visible sign, so that the people may at any moment adore, contemplate, speak and listen to him in the silence of faith. To refuse what he offers us would be to repel his grace and insult him.

Such a reminder of the permanent presence of a consecrated host in the tabernacle refers no doubt to the Ordinary of Chapter 95 of the Roman Instruction *Inter Oecumenici* of September 26, 1964. Nevertheless, apart from the institution of viaticum for the sick, such a particular devotion shows a very debatable archaism and seems to deny the value of the development of sacramental theology during the last centuries and to encourage certain deviations that ought to be rightly explained. In the present period of liturgical renewal, many experiences and experiments must be regarded with caution. Criticism can and must be made, as long as it is well founded. It should, above all, prevent any interpretation that might be disrespectful toward the blessed sacrament.

In what follows I wish to make some suggestions concerning the unjustified insistence on two customs unknown by the old tradition, and irreconcilable with the declared principles of a sacramental renewal and of an active participation of the eucharistic community in the great mystery of our salvation. From our point of view these two points are essential, because neither the custom of "private" Masses nor the devotion to the sacrament reserved in the tabernacle can be justified.

PRIVATE MASSES: AN OUT-OF-DATE PRACTICE

When the Early Church composed her liturgical prayers she knew that the faithful were not isolated individuals. A body broken up into fragments was unthinkable for the great Doctors of the Church, so strongly did they feel that they were one body of which the members were closely linked together. According to St. Basil, all these members "are gathered by the Lord himself, who incorporates them one by one into the Church according to their dignity and worth".[1] Precisely this fact (that all members are integrated in the Church) is the reason why every member, lay or clerical, has a charismatic quality. Developing the typological image of the vine used by Christ, St. Basil adds: "All the baptized are the branches of the vine and, grafted upon Christ, bear fruit in him."[2] Moreover, etymologically speaking, the word "liturgy" means a common action of the people in the

[1] *Commentary on Isaiah* 13, 258 (*Patr. Gr.* 30, 572).
[2] *Moralia* 80, 3 (*P.G.* 31, 861).

realm of grace or of sacrifice (*leitos-ergon: laos-ergon*). This action is preeminently the action of the people, of the body and the head, constituting together a mystical unity that offers itself, sanctifies itself and, by perpetuating Calvary, shows its identity and homogeneity in this way.

By his ordination the priest is the visible instrument through which the eucharistic rite is celebrated for the benefit of the faithful and for himself among the faithful. When celebrating the Lord's Supper he renews the miracle of Pentecost. The Holy Spirit descends again and is present among those called together in Christ's name. They are not a gathering of static spectators when the presence of the Spirit is manifested by the consecration of the species and their transformation into divine nourishment.

In such circumstances it is easy to understand how the celebrant plays his part as mediator between the People of God and Christ sacrificed. By mandate of the Church the priest administers the sacrament for the benefit of the people and quite naturally sets the example by taking part in it himself first. He is the mediator of the one and only mediator, Jesus Christ. The relations between the celebrating priest, the act of the eucharist and the partaking faithful have always been conceived in this sense.

Consequently, a eucharistic celebration without a certain assistance of the people does not make sense because its very essence implies the presence of the faithful. The celebration of the eucharist, therefore, without the participation of people constitutes a grave deviation. To realize this it is enough to remind ourselves of the allegorical images that the Fathers used when speaking of the similarities between the formation of the eucharistic bread composed, according to St. Cyprian for example, of small grains and that of the eucharistic gathering composed of the faithful. Both are equally offered at the altar.[3] Since the eucharist is in its very essence an offering not only of the two species but also of the gathering of the faithful, it is a contradiction to talk of the eucharist as possible without the presence of such a gathering.

[3] *Epist.* 62, 13 (*P.L.* 4, 384).

For these reasons the "private" Mass has never been understood or even imagined in the East. For the Orthodox Churches a priest cannot celebrate the eucharist without the gathering of the faithful, since the two species of the eucharist are offered by the faithful and for their own benefit through the priest in order to reach the mystical Head of the Church.

Another consideration: it is precisely this communal aspect of the eucharist that excludes the possibility of celebrating solely for reasons of personal and individual piety on the part of the celebrant. We should not forget that even the great hermits and ascetics, living for long periods apart from their community, never celebrated the liturgy for themselves. On the contrary, they betook themselves periodically to their central church to obtain the holy sacrament which they then took along with them. Thus, while excluding any thought of even the possibility of a "private" Mass, they could nourish their soul with the body and blood of the Lord in their solitude.

From the Orthodox point of view, if the practice of the "private" Mass is insisted upon, there is a very great danger of losing the meaning of the offering as a communal action and the whole communal meaning of the eucharist. It has often been said that the purpose of the Mass is simultaneously communion (*koinonia*) with God (*theosis*) and communion with neighbor. But how can this purpose be achieved if the faithful are not present? [4]

I would even say that it seems possible that the present liturgical crisis and the weakening of the sense of brotherhood among Christians may be due to this deviation of the "private" Mass.

By severing oneself from the one and only great meal of the

---

[4] The Fathers saw the eucharist as preeminently the sacrament that sanctifies and leads to theosis. "Human nature shares in immortality through visible means and thus passes into the heavenly world" (Gregory of Nyssa, *P.G.* 45, 97). "The divine fire consumes our sins and by this communion makes us divine" (John Damasc., *P.G.* 94, 1149). We must remember that the great Doctors insisted in their teaching on the fact that the eucharist led to theosis in order to defend the doctrine of the hypostatic union of the two natures. We can attain the divinization of our human nature because Christ first took on human nature and divinized it in his incarnation.

whole family of the local Christian community, one is gradually led to isolated and occasionally completely "private" services. But early Christian archaeology proves that the first churches had only one altar. The early Christians did not want several or even only two altars in different places to break up the organic unity of the one meal.

The image of one common meal, reflecting the one Supper of the Lord, predominates in all the frescos of the catacombs and in all the Byzantine churches. If I might give my personal opinion I would say that, since the Council has approved concelebration, I would like to see one single concelebration for all the celebrating priests in a given church on certain days. This would strengthen the bonds of love and communion and would show that there is only one meal around one table. We hope that the number of additional altars in the churches be cut down so that the presence of one single altar can bring out in full relief the grandeur of the eucharist, uniting all the faithful in one family, gathered around one or more celebrating fathers. This is nothing new; rather is it the return to those ancient customs that the Orthodox liturgical tradition has so carefully preserved.

In this connection one should also take into account the inner structure and the vocabulary of the eucharistic text, always conceived in terms of a total offering of the congregation with Christ sacrificed. I cannot analyze this here but neither this structure nor the vocabulary, always in the plural, can be reconciled with the "private" Mass. The absence of a gathering of faithful, and therefore the absence of the body of Christ, brings with it a lack of symmetry and of liturgical balance because, without the eucharistic gathering one has the head, Christ, who offers himself, without the other members of the mystical body.

The first Supper of Maundy Thursday was celebrated in the presence of the disciples, and this fact implies the presence of guests at every eucharistic meal. This meal was probably based on the Jewish rite where the father of the family took the cup of wine mixed with a little water, blessed it and drank of it. Then every guest drank of it in turn. This is probably the cup, St. Luke

(22, 17) tells us, that Christ blessed at the beginning of the Supper.

The celebrating priest, therefore, always takes the place of the father of the family. The celebration of the eucharist is inconceivable if the father is not surrounded by his children or members of the family. They are an essential and organic part of the whole procedure. If they are absent, the family loses its character, its unity, its basic feature; it even loses the very essence of what Christ intended when instituting the meal where he would be surrounded and assisted by all those who express the makeup of a genuine, human family.

DEVOTION TO THE RESERVED EUCHARIST WAS UNKNOWN IN THE EARLY CHURCH

When the text of the Encyclical speaks of the sacraments, it generally tends to consider them too much as simple ritual regulations that must be treated with respect. It suffers from a certain legalism and ritualism. Yet, the Church has always maintained that the sacrament is always necessary for man because of the utter weakness of man who needs grace. Now, in the sacrament we have a powerful means, always at our disposal, adapted to our human nature and infinitely efficacious. Any other presentation of the sacrament runs the danger of creating a static and less creative image, a conception which does not see that the sacrament profoundly affects the whole man, his will, his spirit. And if the sacrament does not influence the whole man, it does not produce the desired results in him.

There is the danger that ultimately, in practice, the sacrament may become a folkloristic custom among so many others. It is then very difficult for a nonbeliever to understand the transformation that takes place in it, to see the communal and saving role of the eucharist, and the concrete contribution it makes to the spiritual life of man. We should also remember the warning given by Christ about worship: "So if you are offering your gift at the altar, and there remember that your brother has something against you, leave your gift there before the altar and go; first be reconciled to your brother, and then come and offer your gift" (Matt. 5, 23-24). Sacrifice and prayer are linked with the cleansing of the inner man of all hatred, quarrels with the neighbor and all influence of the evil one. The reconciliation with the brother precedes the offering of the gift. And thus reconciliation, peace and love on the local social level, are presented as the consequences of a genuine liturgical life.

Let us not forget that the Christian people, redeemed and saved, must become in turn a people for the renewal and salvation of others. The Christian community's dynamic force and influence on the life exterior to it are linked with the sacramental life. On this point the whole teaching can be reduced to a single phrase: man's cooperation with God. This means that he who receives the sacrament receives in it immense possibilities for working with God for the transfiguration of the world. Here, such teachings as that of Christ's universal kingship find their natural context.

Byzantine theology has never been troubled by quarrels about the real presence. Occasionally one finds an allusion in certain liturgical authors to the real presence and the transformation of the two species into the body and blood of Christ. For example, St. Simeon the New Theologian, Archbishop of Salonika in the 15th century, says: "In truth, this is a great mystery—God among men, God among gods deified by the divinity of the true God who is God by nature." [5]

In the East, the sacrament reserved in the tabernacle or in the ciborium has never become the object of a particular and isolated devotion. The rubrics know nothing whatsoever about prayers and processions in honor of the eucharist. There is, of course, the problem of the liturgy of the Pre-Sanctified. But even in this case, the custom must be seen in the light of the old mentality that looked on the Wednesday and Friday of Holy Week as days of Lent, and therefore as days without a liturgy, and the sacra-

[5] *On the Liturgy* 94 (*P.G.* 155, 286).

ment already consecrated on the previous Sunday was used for the celebration of the eucharist.

The 2nd canon of the Council of Antioch (341) disapproved of those who practiced a special devotion to the blessed sacrament without having received it at the celebration of the eucharist. The man who indulged in this practice would be, according to St. John Chrysostom, like a man who, having accepted an invitation to come to a meal and having washed his hands, would refuse to eat.[6]

On the other hand, it is an undeniable fact that in the East, in early times, the Church never refused to use the reserved eucharist for the sick, the prisoners and those who were in special need of it. As Metrophanes Critopoulos, Patriarch of Alexandria (1589), said: "We maintain that the reserved sacrament remains always sacred without losing any of its sacredness."[7]

Now let us look at the question of frequent communion. St. Basil of Caesarea advocated this practice and himself received communion at least four times a week. He wrote: "To communicate, even every day, and to receive one's share in the holy body and precious blood of Christ is a good and profitable thing. 'He who eats my flesh and drinks my blood has eternal life.' Who can doubt, indeed, that to partake constantly of life is the same as to live fully?"[8] In order to make frequent communion possible for the faithful, they could, in the days of St. Basil, take the eucharist with them and take it themselves with their own hands in the absence of a priest.

And there is another point that can throw light on this question: the problem of what had to be done with the sacred species remaining after the communion of the faithful. A historian of the 11th century, Nicephorus Callistus, says that in order to avoid the disintegration of the consecrated particles by time and humidity or their being thrown away, they were rather given to children to eat.[9] The 6th-century historian, Evagrius, confirms

---

[6] *Hom. III on the Ephesians* (*P.G.* 62, 29).
[7] *Confession*, 9.
[8] *Letter 93* (*P.G.* 32, 485).
[9] *Hist. Eccl.* 17, 25 (*P.G.* 147, 281).

that the remains were sometimes distributed so that they might be consumed by small children who were innocent because of their age.[10] There were also cases, though very rare, where the remains of the sacrament were burned. It seems that one preferred to practice the precept of the Old Testament: "And what remains of the flesh and the bread you shall burn with fire" (Lev. 8, 32), if there was any danger of these remains being exposed to deterioration. Neither Hippolytus nor any Doctor of the early Church maintained the thesis of *Mysterium Fidei* that the remains of the sacrament must be worshiped with solemnity by the faithful outside the celebration of the eucharistic liturgy. The texts mentioned in the Encyclical are well chosen but badly applied because they refer to times of persecution, and to exceptional periods, and in no way encourage adoration as the Encyclical does.[11]

CONCLUSIONS

The best way to understand a truth is to live it, "veritatem facere". Now, in the communal liturgical celebration we "do the truth" essentially and eminently.

A teaching on the liturgy that would neglect this vital aspect and limit itself to external factors by describing the order, history and archaeological source without adequate reference to the didactic and catechetical aspect, would depart from the true message and principal aim of the sacrament. To understand and celebrate the liturgy rightly, a systematic and well-developed teaching is required. The eucharistic celebration is a constitutive element in the inner development of the faith. *Lex orandi, lex credendi* (the law of prayer is the law of faith) is a maxim that has been strongly emphasized in the East and has been particularly developed by St. Gregory Nazianzen.

In a human and divine organism like the Church which attempts to reach every soul while taking their individual defects

[10] *Ibid.*, 4, 36 (*P.G.* 86, 2769).
[11] B. Botte, *La Tradition Apostolique de St. Hippolyte*, p. 84.

into account, the forms remain at the service of what is basic, the divine message which these forms must transmit. These forms must therefore be capable of renewal and diversity in order to meet the needs that inevitably change and vary. Therefore, however beautiful and moving and venerable certain forms of the liturgy may appear to us, one should beware of pretending to perpetuate, universalize and sacralize them forever. For these forms reflect the religious and theological climate and needs of a specific period which is bound to pass.

All that has been said should not be interpreted as implying the denial or disapproval of the past—far from it—but it is rather an appeal for a more noble and more edifying conception for the sake of the People of God. I have the impression that the restoration and renewal of the liturgy, decided upon by Vatican Council II, might bring about the abolition of rites that recall the sad and controversial days of the Counter-Reformation and were therefore wholly temporary in character.[12] But to go back to usages that have arisen for reasons that are no longer valid seems to me to show a certain liturgical rigorism in contradiction with the widely proclaimed spirit of *aggiornamento*.

[12] See the arguments against certain usages and the explanation of some regrettable deviations given by Dom Lambert Beaudouin, in *Mélanges liturgiques* (Louvain, 1954).

BIOGRAPHICAL NOTES

HANS KÜNG: Born March 19, 1928, in Switzerland, he was ordained in 1954 for the diocese of Basel. He studied at the Gregorian University in Rome and the Institut Catholique of the Sorbonne in Paris. He earned his doctorate in theology from the Sorbonne in 1957. There followed two years as vicar at Hofkirche, Lucerne, Switzerland, and a year as an assistant at the University of Münster, W. Germany. In 1960 he became professor of fundamental theology at Tübingen University, W. Germany, and three years later was appointed to his present post as professor of dogmatic and ecumenical theology, and director of the Institute of Ecumenical Theology at Tübingen. He was a *peritus* at Vatican Council II. His published works include *Council, Reform and Reunion, That the World May Believe, The Council in Action, Structures of the Church* and *Justification*.

ERWIN ISERLOH: Born May 15, 1915, in Duisburg, W. Germany, he was ordained in 1940. He pursued his studies at the Universities of Münster and Bonn, where he earned a doctorate in theology. He lectured at the University of Bonn before being appointed to the post of Director of the Münster Social Academy. Since 1954 he has taught medieval and modern Church history in the Theological Faculty at Trèves, France. His published works include *Gnade und Eucharistie in der Theologie des Wilhelm v. Ockham* (1956), *Abendmahl und Opfer* (1960), and *Luthers Thesenanschlag—Tatsache oder Legende?* (1962). He is also a contributor to theological reviews.

ERNST WOLF: Born August 2, 1902, in Prague. He joined the German Evangelical Church, and studied at the Universities of Vienna, Rostock, Leipzig and Göttingen. He earned his licentiate in theology in 1925, and holds honorary doctorates in theology from the University of Rostock, the Free Faculty of Protestant Theology, Paris, and the University of Vienna. He is President of the Evangelical Theology Society, directs the Commission for the History of Inter-Church Dissension, and at present teaches systematic theology and Church history at the University of Göttingen.

JEAN BOSC: Born October 31, 1910, in Lille, France. He studied at the Universities of Lille, Frankfurt, Paris and Bonn, earning his licentiate in letters and his doctorate in theology. He is at present professor of dogmatic theology in the Free Faculty of Protestant Theology at the University of Paris, a member of the National Council of the French Reformed Church, and Director of *Foi et Vie*. Among his published works are *L'Unité dans le Seigneur* (1964) and *La Foi chrétienne* (1965).

ALEXANDRE GANOCZY: Born December 12, 1928, in Budapest, he was ordained in 1953. He is a naturalized French citizen. He studied at Pazmány University in Budapest, the Institut Catholique in Paris, the Gregorian University in Rome, and at the Mainz Institute of European

History, earning his doctorate in theology. He was chaplain to Hungarian refugees in France from 1955 to 1961, and is at present Hans Küng's assistant at the Institute of Ecumenical Research at the University of Tübingen. This fall he will join the Institut Catholique in Paris as a lecturer in sacramental theology. His published works include *Calvin und Vatikanum II. Das Problem der Kollegialitat* (1965). He is a regular contributor to a number of reviews.

BONIFACE A. WILLEMS, O.P.: Born December 4, 1926, in Rotterdam, the Netherlands. He became a Dominican, studied at Zwolle and Nijmegen, and was ordained in 1952. Further studies followed at the Universities of Münster, Basle and Straatsburg. He earned his doctorate at the University of Münster in 1957. At present he is professor of dogmatic theology at the Albertinum in Nijmegen, the Netherlands. His theological interests are shown in many articles about the Church, as well as in his writings about such personalities as Karl Barth and Karl Jaspers: cf. his book *Karl Barth* (1963), and the collective work *Mens en God* (1963).

GOTTHOLD HASENHÜTTL: Born December 2, 1933, in Graz, Austria, he was ordained in 1959. He studied at the Universities of Graz, Rome, Marburg and Tübingen, earning his doctorate in theology in 1962. He was assigned to parish work until 1964 when he was made an assistant in the Institute of Ecumenical Research at the University of Tübingen. His published works include *Der Glaubensvollzug: Eine Begegnung mit R. Bultmann aus Katholischen Glaubensverständnis,* and he is an active contributor to various theological reviews.

HAMILCAR ALIVISATOS: Born May 17, 1887, in Cefallonia, Greece. He studied at the University and Academy of Athens, earning a degree in theology in 1907. He holds honorary doctorates in theology from the Universities of Oxford, Salonika, Moscow and Uppsala. At one time he was Director of a department at the Ministry of Religious Affairs and National Education, and professor of canon law at the University of Athens. At present he is Procurator of the Holy Synod, and an active member of the Academy of Athens. His published works include *Kaiser Justinians kirchliche Gesetzgebung* (1913), *The Canons of the Orthodox Church* and many other books on canon law, history and liturgy. He is a frequent contributor to reviews, and at present is engaged in studies on the ecclesiastical law of the Orthodox Church and on the ecumenical question.

PAUL EVDOKIMOV: Born August 1, 1901, in St. Petersburg. He studied at the University of Aix en Provence and the St. Serge Institute of Orthodox Theology, where he is presently a professor. His numerous published works include *Les Ages de la Vie Spirituelle* (1961), *L'Orthodoxie* (1959), and *La Femme et le Salut du Monde* (1958). He contributes regularly to various reviews, including *Irénikon, Lumière et Vie, Verbum Caro, Kerygma und Dogma* and *La Vie Spirituelle.*

ARTHUR M. ALLCHIN: Born April 20, 1930, in London, he was ordained in the Anglican Church in 1957. He studied at Christ Church College, Oxford and Cuddesdon Theological College, Oxford. At one time vicar of St. Mary Abbots in Kensington, he is at present librarian and prefect of studies at Pusey House, Oxford. His published works include *The Silent Rebellion: Anglican Religious Communities, 1845-1900* (1963), *Newman, A Portrait Restored* (1965) and *We Belong to One Another: Methodist, Anglican and Orthodox Essays* (ed.) (1965). He is an active contributor to various reviews, particularly on ecumenical subjects.

FRANKLIN LITTELL: Born June 20, 1917, in Syracuse, New York, he was ordained in the Methodist Church in 1941. He studied at Cornell University, Union Theological Seminary and Yale University, earning his licentiate in letters and philosophy in 1940 and his doctorate in theology in 1947. He also holds an honorary doctorate in theology from the University of Marburg. At present he is professor of Church history at the Chicago Theological Seminary, and is a member of the Rock River Conference of the Methodist Church. His published works include *The Free Church* (1957), *The Anabaptist View of the Church* (1958), *The German Phoenix* (1960), *From State Church to Pluralism* and *A Tribute to Menno Simons* (1961).

DANIEL J. O'HANLON, S.J.: Born in 1919, he became a Jesuit in 1939 and was ordained in 1952. He studied at Loyola University in Los Angeles, in the Philosophical Faculty of Gonzaga University in the State of Washington, the Gregorian University in Rome, and at the Universities of Dublin, Fribourg and Tübingen, earning doctorates in philosophy and in theology. A specialist in ecumenical questions, he co-edited with Yves Congar and Hans Küng *The Council Speeches of Vatican II* (1964), and he is also co-editor of *Christianity Divided*. He is a regular contributor to such publications as *Theological Studies, Cross Currents, Worship, Commonweal* and *America*.

JORGE MEJÍA: Born in Buenos Aires, he was ordained in 1945. He studied at the Collegium Angelicum and the Biblical Institute in Rome, earning a degree in Bible sciences in 1950 and a doctorate in theology in 1956. He is at present professor of Scripture at the Argentine Catholic University, where he is also secretary of the Theology Faculty. His published works include *Pequena Historia de la Biblia* (1964), and he contributes regularly to *Lumen Vitae, The Ecumenist, Estudios Biblicos,* and to *Criterio* of which he is editor.

MAURICE VILLAIN, S.M.: He became a Marist, and was ordained at the age of 27. He studied at the Sorbonne, l'Ecole des Chartes, l'Ecole des Hautes Etudes, the Collegium Angelicum, and in the Theology Faculty of Lyons, earning his doctorate in theology in 1929. He taught dogmatic theology from 1929 to 1932, and Church history from 1932 to 1949. His published works include *La prière de Jésus pour l'Unité chrétienne, La Vocation de l'Eglise* and *Oécumenisme spirituel*. He is a regular contributor to various theological reviews.

HILAIRE MAROT, O.S.B.: Born October 14, 1920, he became a Benedictine, and pursued his studies at the University of Paris and at the Collegio San Anselmo in Rome, earning degrees in theology and history.

He is a regular contributor to various reviews, notably *Irénikon,* and has contributed to several symposia.

VILMOS VAJTA: Born June 15, 1918, in Hungary, he was ordained in the Lutheran Church in 1940. He studied in the theological faculties of Sopron, Uppsala and Lund, and earned his doctorate in theology in 1952. At present he is professor of research at the Center of Ecumenical Studies in Strasbourg, and is widely known for his work as director of the theology department of the World Lutheran Federation in Geneva. His many published works include *Kirche und Abendmahl* (1963) and *Gelebte Rechtfertigung* (1963), in addition to regular contributions to Lutheran reviews.

METROPOLITAN EMILIANOS TIMIADIS: Born in 1917 in Iconium, Turkey, he studied at the Theological School of Constantinople and at Oxford University, earning a degree in theology at Chalki. Archimandrite and Bishop, he did parish work in Constantinople from 1941 to 1946, in England from 1947 to 1952, and in Belgium from 1952 to 1959. In 1961 he became Metropolitan of Calabre. At present he is a representative of the Ecumenical Patriarch to the World Council of Churches. His published works include a number of books, mostly in Greek, and contributions to various reviews, including *Una Sancta, Schweizer Monatshefte, Verbum Caro* and *Ecclesia.* He is engaged in studies on birth control, indulgences, the therapeutic character of penance, and the problems of the Pan-Orthodox Assembly.

International Publishers of CONCILIUM

ENGLISH EDITION
Paulist Press
Glen Rock, N. J., U.S.A.
Burns & Oates Ltd.
25 Ashley Place
London, S.W.1

DUTCH EDITION
Uitgeverij Paul Brand, N. V.
Hilversum, Netherlands

FRENCH EDITION
Maison Mame
Tours/Paris, France

GERMAN EDITION
Verlagsanstalt Benziger & Co., A.G.
Einsiedeln, Switzerland
Matthias Grunewald-Verlag
Mainz, W. Germany

SPANISH EDITION
Ediciones Guadarrama
Madrid, Spain

PORTUGUESE EDITION
Livraria Morais Editora, Ltda.
Lisbon, Portugal

ITALIAN EDITION
Editrice Queriniana
Brescia, Italy